Conten

G000130946

FIGURES

TABLES

Acknowledgements

I wish to thank Professor R.V. Comerford and the teaching staff of the Department of Modern History, NUI, Maynooth, in particular Dr Raymond Gillespie for his encouragement and support throughout the preparation of this publication. I record my indebtedness to the West Yorkshire Archive Service, Leeds, for permission to include material from Clanricarde's letters and to the staffs of the following repositories: the Public Record Office, London, the Bodleian Library, University of Oxford, the National Archives, the National Library of Ireland, the NUI Maynooth Library, the James Hardiman Library, NUIG, and Galway County Library.

I thank my colleague, Martin Joseph Clarke, whose constant support is much appreciated. I acknowledge the valuable suggestions of my friends, Dr Ian Clark (Canada), Christy Cunniffe, John Dillon, Mary Fahy, Thomas Feeney, Joseph Forde, Ultan Hynes, Michael McMahon, Ursula Mooney, Stephen Nevin, Mary Burke and Fr Declan Kelly. Finally, I wish to thank my wife, Mary, and our two children, Lisa and James, for their patience and understanding throughout. To them I dedicate this work.

Maynooth Studies in Local History: Number 47

A Galway landlord during the Great Famine

Ulick John de Burgh, first marquis of Clanricarde

John Joseph Conwell

FOUR COURTS PRESS

Set in 10pt on 12pt Bembo by
Carrigboy Typesetting Services, County Cork for
FOUR COURTS PRESS LTD
7 Malpas Street, Dublin 8, Ireland
e-mail: info@four-courts-press.ie
http://www.four-courts-press.ie
and in North America for
FOUR COURTS PRESS
c/o ISBS, 920 N.E. 58th Avenue, Suite 300, Portland, OR 97213.

ISBN 1–85182–762–5

Printed in Ireland by
ßetaprint Ltd, Dublin

Introduction

As a politician and landowner Ulick John de Burgh (1802–74), marquis of Clanricarde, moved in two distinct and separate worlds, straddling two different countries and cultures. This short book examines his role as a cabinet minister (1846–52) and as a major Galway landowner, with emphasis on his contribution to, and attitude towards, government policies on Ireland in the years prior to, and during, the Great Famine. The study also assesses the immediate and long-term effects of the Famine on his 52,000-acre estate in Co. Galway. When he entered the cabinet, the marquis was presented with an opportunity to influence government policy on Ireland during the Famine. This study sets out to analyze his performance. It examines the contradictions which existed between his public rhetoric as a national political figure and the implementation of government policies at local level in east Galway. Clanricarde is an interesting subject for research because, to date, no detailed study has been undertaken on this wealthy Irish landed magnate and politician who possessed all the necessary pedigree and status to secure high political office. Only passing reference has been made to him in previously published works on the Famine period by Donnelly,[1] Gray,[2] Kerr[3] and Kinealy.[4]

The crisis precipitated by the Famine brought into sharp focus the political beliefs and philosophies of contemporary political figures and crystallized their attitudes on a range of issues such as poor law, Famine relief measures, religion, estate management, land tenure and evictions. An assessment of Clanricarde's performance in relation to these matters further contributes to the historiography of Famine period.

Much of the primary source material for this work is located in the Clanricarde papers held at the West Yorkshire Archive Service in Leeds. This collection contains correspondence between the marquis, several Galway landowners and contemporary politicians. Clanricarde's correspondence with the prime minister provides an insight into the working of the British cabinet during the Famine period. This extensive collection of letters, deposited in the Public Record Office in London, addresses several Famine-related matters and reveals Clanricarde's opinions of many of his political contemporaries. His letters to Clarendon, the Irish lord lieutenant, address many of these same issues and are deposited in the Bodleian Library in Oxford University. The many contributions of Clanricarde to House of Lords debates are to be found in the third series of *Hansard*.

Most of Clanricarde's Galway property lay within the Loughrea poor law union. The Parliamentary Papers contain primary printed material relating to that union and its workhouse, focusing on an extensive inquiry conducted there in 1848 by a poor law inspector when vice guardians were appointed to run that union's affairs. The manuscript correspondence between Clanricarde and the relief commission is housed in the National Archives in Dublin, as are the documented reports on the Famine by state officials and the correspondence of private individuals. These provided most useful evidence of the Famine's impact on Clanricarde's estate. The census reports are used to analyse the demographic change on Clanricarde's property during, and subsequent to, the Famine period. While no estate records survive, it is, nonetheless, possible to build up a fairly comprehensive picture of the deterioration that occurred there during the Famine.

Local newspapers from the period such as the *Tuam Herald*, the *Galway Vindicator*, the *Galway Advertiser* and the *Western Star* give accounts of events from a local perspective. Relevant reports in the British and Irish newspapers, *The Times*, *The Nation*, the *Illustrated London News* and the *Freeman's Journal* representing all sides of political opinion, set events in a broader context and helped to provide a more complete discussion of the issues involved. The oral evidence gathered in videotaped interviews from seventy local people provided information not to be found in any documented source and added to the understanding of how Clanricarde and the Famine were perceived at local level.

1. The first marquis of Clanricarde, 1802–74

A general knowledge of the Clanricarde family background is necessary to gain perspective on the place and standing of Ulick John de Burgh in Co. Galway and his political connections which contributed to his appointment as a cabinet minister during the Famine years. The de Burgos (later de Burghs and Burkes), who became earls of Clanricarde, were of Norman ancestry. William de Burgo, who came to Ireland with King John in 1185, married the daughter of Donal Mór O'Brien, king of Thomond, and was granted huge tracts of land in Munster. He crossed into Connacht in 1203 and established strongholds on the banks of the river Shannon at Meelick and Portumna. His son Richard, made lord of Connacht by King John, was granted almost all the land of that province by charter in 1226, with the exception of five cantreds near Athlone. He based his headquarters at Loughrea, thus beginning the family's 700-year association with Co. Galway. In 1265, the family acquired through marriage the earldom of Ulster so that, for a time, the de Burgos owned more land in Ireland than the king of England himself.[1] William, the 'Brown' earl, was murdered in Carrickfergus in 1333; in 1352, his only child, Elizabeth, married Lionel, duke of Clarence, son of Edward III. Richard, duke of York, father of King Edward IV, was descended from this marriage, forming a royal connection with the de Burgh family.

By his marriage to the heiress of the 'Brown earl', Lionel became lord of Connacht and fourth earl of Ulster. However, he was not allowed to exercise his claim over his territory in the west of Ireland, as the descendants of a junior branch of the family, represented by William Liath de Burgh, took possession of their ancestral lands in Connacht. William's two sons, Ulick and Edmund, divided these lands into two great lordships. Edmund settled in the northern portion and became ancestor to the Burkes of Mayo, while Ulick took possession of the Galway lands and founded the Clanricarde branch of the family. Neither Edmund nor Ulick displayed any allegiance to the crown and lived in the style of Gaelic chieftains in their manners, language and dress. Their descendants continued to rule in this fashion for over two hundred years until the accession to power of Henry VIII.

On 1 July 1543, Ulick de Burgh, who was the then head of the Galway branch of the family, submitted to the king and received the title of earl of Clanricarde, together with a grant of the land of six baronies in the county. By this move the Clanricardes changed from being warlords to landlords and remained loyal to the crown, becoming one of the most powerful and influential families in Ireland.[2] Richard, the fourth earl, was knighted on the battlefield, having fought against the Irish at Kinsale. President of Connacht between 1604 and 1616 and governor of Galway in the latter years of his presidency, he married Frances Walsingham, a wealthy, well-connected English heiress; he had the means to build a substantial residence at Somerhill, in Kent where he also owned considerable property; such was his standing with the English establishment that, in 1629, he was also conferred with the earldom of St Albans in the English peerage, a title superior in English eyes to his Irish one, and a unique achievement for an Irish peer.

Sometime before 1618 he built his Irish seat, Portumna Castle, an imposing semi-fortified mansion at a cost of £10,000 (fig. 1). Situated on the shores of Lough Derg, and positioned within a demesne of 1400 acres, it faced north-wards onto the territory in which successive earls of Clanricarde wielded their considerable authority. The demesne itself was bounded by a high limestone wall, constructed during the Famine, and physically symbolized the barrier which then existed between the social classes, with the wealthy aristocratic family on the inside and the impoverished peasantry on the outside.

Ulick, the 5th earl, played a distinguished and conspicuous part in Irish affairs during the turbulent period between the outbreak of rebellion in 1641 and the Cromwellian conquest. Although a devout Catholic, he was a confirmed royalist, and used his strategically influential position between the royalist government and the Irish Catholics to the king's advantage.[3] His Galway lands were confiscated by Cromwell but restored to the family under Charles II, only to be forfeited again after the battle of Aughrim. In 1689, Richard, the 8th earl of Clanricarde, commanded a regiment in the army of King James but surrendered the town of Galway to Ginkel. His brother, Ulick, lost his life while fighting on the side of James at Aughrim, while another brother, John, also fought at Aughrim and later became the 9th earl. In 1704, the Clanricarde lands were returned to John, only after he had agreed to conform to the established religion and to pay a fine of £25,000. John's sister, Honora, married the Jacobite general, Patrick Sarsfield, earl of Lucan, at the Dominican priory in Portumna, probably in 1691; two years after Sarsfield's death at the battle of Landen in 1693, she married James, duke of Berwick, eldest natural son of James II.[4]

John's son, Michael, on succeeding his father in 1722, also conformed to the established church, and from this point onwards, the family fulfilled a typical ascendancy role. In 1793, John Thomas de Burgh, the 13 earl, raised a regiment known as the 'Connaught Rangers' and for over one hundred years men from this celebrated group fought for the empire in Europe, Asia and South Africa.[5] Portumna castle was accidentally destroyed by fire in 1826 when Ulick John, the 14th earl, was 24 years of age. Most of its contents, including estate and family documents, were destroyed. Only a small amount

1 Portumna castle, seat of the Clanricardes, built before 1618. Destroyed by fire in 1826 and under restoration by the state in 2002.

of furniture and a few valuable paintings were saved. The family then moved to out-offices, fitted up as a temporary residence.[6]

This outline of the Clanricarde lineage serves to demonstrate that Ulick John de Burgh possessed all the necessary pedigree, wealth and status to become a major political figure and represent the elitist class to which he belonged.

Ulick John de Burgh,[7] only son of the protestant John Thomas de Burgh, 13th earl of Clanricarde, and Elizabeth Burke, a Catholic from the neighbouring Marble Hill estate, was born at Belmont in Hampshire, on 28 December 1802. Raised as a protestant son of this mixed marriage, he inherited the Clanricarde title as a minor on the death of his father in 1808. He spent much of his early life at the family seat at Portumna where governesses educated him, before he progressed to a more formal education at Eton (1814–18).[8] He matriculated into Oxford on 16 October 1820, but there is no record of his graduating from there.[9] The young Clanricarde was described as 'good-looking, clever and very gentlemanlike as well as being immensely rich'.[10] He developed a love of hunting and horseracing during his years at Eton and

Oxford, and William Gregory described him as the best man to hounds he
had ever seen.[11] During the middle decades of the 19th century, Clanricarde,
his son, Lord Dunkellin, and Gregory were among the best-known horseracing enthusiasts in the British Isles.

His status in life was further enhanced by his marriage, in April 1825, to
Harriet, daughter of George Canning, foreign secretary and later, in 1827,
prime minister.[12] Much of later Clanricarde's political advancement was due
to this matrimonial alliance. In November 1825, he was raised a step in the
peerage to assume the title, of marquis of Clanricarde, and by December 1826
he had become Baron Somerhill in the English peerage. He served as under-
secretary of state for foreign affairs from 1826 to 1827 when he resigned from
that position.[13] He became a privy councillor in 1830 and held the ceremo-
nial appointment of captain of the yeomen of the guard from 1830 to 1834.[14]

In 1838, at the age of 36, he was appointed British ambassador to Russia
and he and Lady Clanricarde spent the following three years in St Petersburg.
This posting was due, in part, to the influence of his friend and fellow Irish
landowner, Lord Palmerston, who was foreign secretary.[15] Clanricarde lost his
position as ambassador when the Tories returned to power in 1841. In 1846,
he gained political office once more, when he was appointed to serve in Lord
John Russell's administration as postmaster general. His term in cabinet, until
1852, coincided with the years of the Great Famine in Ireland. His final
government appointment was that of lord privy seal in Palmerston's cabinet.
This lasted only a few weeks in February 1858 and ended with the fall of that
administration.[16]

In his private life Clanricarde had a partiality for socializing and partying
and was criticized for having a fondness for low company.[17] In the mid 1820s,
prior to his marriage to Harriet Canning, an undated, anonymous letter
warned her father about the type of young man he was allowing his daughter
to marry.

> Have you enquired into the character of the man to whom you give
> your daughter? Have you followed him in his buffian career at Eton and
> Oxford? Know you the sources from which he derives his wealth,
> unassailed by poverty or embarrassment? He has had recourse to
> dishonest and disgraceful proceedings ... he is divested of truth, honour
> or honesty ... Give not your child to corruption, pollution and shame.
> Your own downfall must and will be the result.[18]

Clanricarde's relationship with his wife began to deteriorate from an early
stage in their marriage, and although the union produced seven children, the
Irish parliamentarian, T.P. O'Connor, contended that the marriage was
'notoriously unhappy'.

2 Ulick John de Burgh, first marquis of Clanricarde.

I have heard stories of the doings of this formidable, somewhat old-fashioned type of Irish landlord, including a long and fruitful intrigue with the very beautiful daughter of one of his tenants. There were claimants to his parenthood in many instances; one, a great social figure in London well known to Labouchere and all the bloods and wits of that period, played a very popular social role.[19]

Several accounts refer to his extra-marital affairs and memories of his amorous exploits have become engrained in the folklore of east Galway.[20] A survey conducted by this author in the late 1990s, received contributions from seventy senior citizens in the Portumna area, many of whom gave accounts of the various romantic affairs that Clanricarde was believed to have had while he resided at Portumna.[21] That side of Clanricarde's character was also alluded to in an article in the nationalist newspaper, *United Ireland*, in 1886.

Ulick John, the most noble, was not exempt from frailties of the flesh, and he left his present dutiful son a vast number of brothers and sisters whose names are not to be found in the peerage, and left besides quite a miscellaneous assortment of stepmothers. Amongst them was a certain

Mrs S, who had received as the wages of sin a certain small house and patch of ground in the vicinity of Portumna.[22]

Clanricarde's fall from political favour was largely due to his rather bohemian lifestyle. The final scandal which later brought him into political disfavour centred on the *Handcock v. Delacour* court case in 1855 in which it was alleged that Clanricarde had schemed to secure the Handcock inheritance of the Carantrila estate near Tuam for his illegitimate son, Delacour. Clanricarde filed an affidavit with the court of chancery rebutting the imputations made against him, and although no evidence was produced in court that Delacour actually was Clanricarde's son, his strenuous denials were not believed.[23] Despite his attempts to put his own side of the story, Clanricarde's reputation as a public figure in mid-Victorian Britain was irreparably damaged as a result of these revelations.[24] In 1858, *The Times* demanded an explanation of his role in the affair or his withdrawal from the house of lords. It blamed him for the fall of the government, stating that Palmerston's

> chief error was the introduction of Lord Clanricarde into cabinet … this act more than any other measure contributed to his overthrow … a public scandal universally condemned, an outrage on public feeling …[25]

On the domestic political scene, Clanricarde was lord lieutenant of Co. Galway from 1831 until his death in 1874. In that capacity, he acted as the crown's chief representative in the county. The power of local government was vested in him, his deputy lieutenant and magistrates; he appointed the county's high sheriff and presided over social functions, attended by the county's gentry, several of whom sought his political patronage. His position of influence is highlighted by the number of petitions and requests he received from individuals urging him to intercede on their behalf to gain promotions and appointments.[26]

As an active member of the house of lords, he lobbied for Irish interests throughout his political life. He was perceived by many of his fellow Irish landlords to be a man of considerable political ability and was requested to head up an Irish party in 1836.[27] His eldest son, Ulick, Lord Dunkellin, entered politics and won a seat in the 1857 general election to represent Galway borough in the house of commons. From 1865, until his untimely death in 1867, Dunkellin served as MP for the county along with the Tory, William Gregory.[28]

As well as being a significant political figure, Lord Clanricarde was also a major landlord, owning more than 52,000 acres of land, much of it prime quality, in Co. Galway. His estate was comprised of lands in the parishes of Loughrea Portumna, Craughwell, Derrybrien/Ballynakill, Woodford, and Eyrecourt in addition to lands in the environs of Galway town (fig. 3). In

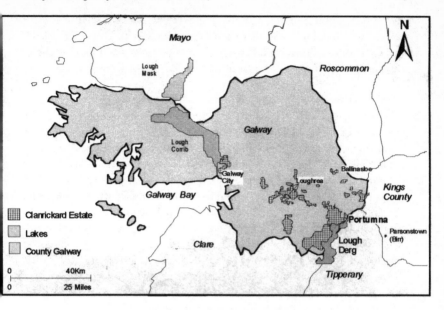

3 Clanricarde's estate in Co. Galway.

1844, his agent revealed to the Devon commission that there were 2,065 tenants on Clanricarde's estate,[29] and according to Griffith's Valuation[30] his property, in 1856, extended into 166 townlands in seven baronies, namely, Longford, Leitrim, Loughrea, Galway, Clonmacnowen, Killconnell and Dunkellin It can also be shown that the east Galway landowners, Clanricarde, Clancarty, Clonbrock and Dunsandle were in possesson of property with a high valuation (Table 1).

Table 1. Major landowners in Co. Galway, 1876

Landowners	Extent in acres	Valuation
Berridge	160,000	£6,300
Clanricarde	52,600	£21,000
Dunsandle	35,500	£21,800
Clonbrock	28,200	£21,400
Clancarty	23,900	£21,750

Clanricarde also owned 4,000 acres of land in England. The income generated from such large estates provided Clanricarde with financial security

and protected him from many of the devastating effects of the Great Famine
which bankrupted many smaller landlords in the west and south of Ireland.
He was, with Lansdowne and Palmerston, part of a very small select group of
wealthy Irish landowners who sat in cabinet during the Great Famine.

In 1838, Melbourne's Liberal government enacted a poor law system for
Ireland similar to the type which already operated in England. One of the
provisions of the poor law legislation was to divide the country into 130
unions, each composed of electoral divisions, and these in turn were made up
of a number of townlands. A board of guardians was to administer each union
and build a workhouse to cater for the union's poor. A poor rate was levied
on the property owners in each union to provide funds for its administration.
The greater part of the Clanricarde estate was included in the Loughrea poor
law union which was declared on 5 September 1839.[31] It comprised an area
of 152,308 acres and had a population of 71,774 in 1841.[32] Its workhouse at
Loughrea, built and furnished at a cost of £8,700 to cater for 800 inmates,
received its first admissions on 26 February 1842.[33] The Loughrea union was
one of six formed in Co. Galway as a result of the 1838 Act, and lesser
portions of the Clanricarde estate lay within the unions of Galway and
Ballinasloe, each having a workhouse to accommodate 1,000 inmates.[34]

For the legislation setting up the Irish poor law system in Ireland was enacted
by a Liberal administration in which Clanricarde served as ambassador to
Russia. From the outset he opposed its introduction and the Irish representatives in both houses of parliament joined him in his opposition to the
system. But despite 86 petitions and 31,221 signatures against its provisions,
the bill passed into law on 31 July 1838.[35]

For a variety of reasons Clanricarde felt unable to support the Bill and he
consistently articulated his several objections to it. In 1838, the *Tuam Herald*
noted that a deputation consisting of Lord Clanricarde and others had an
interview with the duke of Wellington to impress upon him the necessity of
throwing out the measure at its second reading.[36] Clanricarde believed that its
implementation would place excessive rates on already overstretched Irish
landlords and in house of lords debates he stated that they already had a heavy
burden of tithes.[37] He assured his fellow peers that Irish landowners and
gentry believed the bill would be thrown out or materially altered. He knew
that proceedings were already being taken to eject tenants in Ireland as a result
of the alarm that existed there. His objections to the measure were
'interwoven with every clause from preamble to the end'.[38] He argued that
the bill would give the commissioners enormous powers of taxation and that
immense administration expenses must be incurred before relief could be
given to a single person, able bodied or impotent.[39] He believed that the poor
law would be 'detrimental to the moral, the social, and the physical condition

of the people among whom it was introduced'. He suggested that the proposed taxation ought not be limited to only one class of property and felt that such a system would put an end to all public works.[40]

Clanricarde continued to voice his objections to the Act even after its provisions had become law. In seeking returns relative to the working of the poor law in Ireland he stated that 'the expense was so great that it was utterly impossible for that impoverished country to bear it'. The evil of the country was poverty and he thought that the Poor Law bill, instead of diminishing it, would aggravate it.[41] He contended that it was accepted by all sides that if the poor law were to be effective it would require the 'cheerful co-operation and assistance of the people in Ireland'.[42] That had not happened and it had given rise to great discontent and clamour.[43] He went on at length to outline the work of the commissioners who had been appointed in 1834 to enquire into the conditions of the poorer classes in Ireland and referred to their valuable recommendations which had not been implemented.[44] He cited Lord Lansdowne, his fellow Liberal landowner, who, in supporting the introduction of the poor law in 1838, had stated that

> the Bill was necessary on account of clearing of estates, which was proceeding too rapidly, but in others with due caution. Such a measure as this … would deter them [the tenants] from bidding as they now did for estates and also prevent them from feeling so much discontent when ejected by their landlords.[45]

Clanricarde claimed that he had been led to believe the bill was intended to ensure the tranquillity of the country, to put an end to mendicancy, and to lessen the anxiety of the lower orders to obtain land. In a detailed speech to his fellow peers he argued that, in all of these objectives, the poor law had failed dismally. Lansdowne agreed with many of points made by Clanricarde and admitted that it was with the greatest reluctance that he had supported the measure.[46]

In 1844, Clanricarde enquired in the Lords if any bill would be brought forward in that session on the poor law, or if it was proposed to institute any inquiry upon the subject.[47] In the same debate he welcomed the government's intention of spending £60,000 on public works and highlighted the necessity of setting the people to work immediately.[48] The impoverished peasants purchased provisions with the money they earned on the public works until these works were closed down in July 1846. In their place the government introduced a system of locally run soup kitchens to provide food directly to the starving poor in the spring and summer of 1847.[49]

Clanricarde was particularly critical of the way in which the poor law commissioners carried out their duties and in a debate on the workhouses of

Ireland in June 1844, he castigated them for the heavy-handed tactics and expense involved in collecting the poor rates. He cited, as an example, that on one day alone 430 men were employed in a part of Ballinasloe union but had collected only £14. The guardians of the Tuam union did not enforce the payment of the poor rates because they could not get collectors, and the workhouse remained closed although a master, matron, medical officer and porter had been appointed. For similar reasons the workhouses of Ballinasloe, Westport and Ballinrobe had been closed. He suggested that 'if the commissioners had exercised their power in a more mild, temperate and rational manner they might have conciliated the feelings of the people and have obtained the assistance and cooperation of the gentry'.[50]

Clanricarde's continued opposition was once more noted on the eve of the Great Famine when he suggested that a poor law would not be to Ireland's advantage. He claimed to have had petitions from all parts of Ireland stating that mendicancy had increased and that he himself had been a witness to that increase. He contended that the poor law had failed in every respect and had disappointed those who had introduced it.[51]

Clanricarde spent considerable portions of time in Ireland each year and through his various contacts was better informed than most as to the country's needs. He firmly believed that the poor law system was not the most efficient method to tackle the country's problems, and argued that the landed gentry, especially in the unions of the south and west, would be unable to support the disproportionate number of paupers. In campaigning for the implementation of the recommendations of the earlier poor inquiry to relieve the country's increasing social problems he was both far seeing and practical. While it could be argued that he was most anxious to spare himself and his landed class any unnecessary expense in looking after the country's destitute he did realise that the system which operated effectively in Britain could not have the same desired result in Ireland due to the country's overpopulation, poverty and lack of employment opportunities. In holding these views Clanricarde differed little from many leading Irish political figures at the time and he did not lack the courage to articulate his opinions. Such was his outright opposition to the poor law that he was prepared to break with party loyalty and be critical of his own colleagues who had supported the poor law system.

The Clanricarde estate was located in a part of Ireland close to where the Famine had its most devastating and prolonged effects.[52] The initial extent of the potato blight in east Galway was confirmed by the county police inspector, William Lewis, who, having received reports from his sub-inspectors stationed throughout the region for the months of September, October and November 1845, forwarded them to the inspector general at Dublin Castle. The September report for Loughrea district stated that the potato stalks had withered and the rot had become apparent with the potatoes becoming 'a mass of corruption' and having 'an alarming appearance'.[53]

The November report for the sub-district of Marble Hill indicated the naivety of a desperate, panicking population, wanting to believe that divine intervention could provide a cure for the disease.

> Great numbers of persons have left off the digging to go to Scarriff, Co. Clare for the purposes of paying a R.C. clergyman to effect a cure of the diseased potatoes. I directed the constable at Mountshannon to report the extent of their delusions. The constable's report is as follows: 'A report having been circulated that the Revd M. Tuohy, R.C.C. of Scarriff would cure the disease in the potatoes, men and women from several parishes visited and paid him 3*d*. to £1 each for his trouble, amounting to £96 when the Bishop stopped him'.[54]

As lord lieutenant of the county, Clanricarde's opinion was sought by the authorities in Dublin Castle on the extent of the failure of the potato crop and the consequent distress. In a letter to the Irish chief secretary, Sir Thomas Freemantle, in the autumn of 1845, Clanricarde remarked that, having made enquiries, he could confirm that, excluding seed provision, there would be at least a three-month shortage in potato supplies.[55]

During the course of the Famine, government relief efforts in Ireland were implemented in many different phases. Almost immediately, the British prime minister, Sir Robert Peel, reverted to the traditional mechanisms of outdoor relief through local committees, food imports and public works in response to the impending food shortage, despite the existence of a poor law system.[56] In November 1845, a relief commission was set up in Dublin under the chairmanship of Sir Randolph Routh, to advise the government on the extent of distress, organize meal depots throughout the country and to supervise and co-ordinate the activities of the local relief committees.[57] Clanricarde expressed his reservations concerning aspects of the work of the proposed commission in his letter to Freemantle. He disagreed with the proposal of the Irish lord lieutenant, Lord Heytesbury, that public meetings of magistrates, clergy and gentry should be held to instruct the peasantry on best farming practices. He remarked that, despite the efforts of those above them, the peasants lacked the ability to embrace the changes necessary to improve agriculture.

> The peasant is always slow and reluctant to abandon an old and adopt a new system … This cannot easily be done at a public meeting … and if such meetings did not effect good they might be productive of evil. … They might foster a disposition in the lower orders to lean almost wholly upon those above them for support and upon the government and not to attempt extraordinary exertions.[58]

Instead, Clanricarde urged the setting up of local committees with power to aid public works and give employment to the people. He anticipated a worsening of the blight in the potatoes and realized the need for government intervention but did not indicate what form it should take.

> A calamity is impending over the people of this country, to avert which the exertions of individuals or of local committees would prove quite inadequate and which demands the immediate consideration of her majesty's ministers and the early intervention of parliament.[59]

Ironically, the policy of state intervention which he proposed here, is one that the government, of which he himself became a member some months later, was most reluctant to pursue.

In November 1845, Peel authorized the purchase of £100,000 worth of Indian corn from the United States, to be stored in depots throughout Ireland for emergency purposes. Clanricarde, anxious to involve himself in its distribution locally, requested the relief commissioners to set up a corn depot in each of his towns of Portumna and Loughrea, in addition to those already proposed for the towns of Banagher and Galway. He offered the commissioners premises in Portumna for that purpose and suggested that an arrangement might be made with the board of ordnance to permit the corn to be stored in the barracks of those towns. These barracks had been built for cavalry but were now occupied by infantry and were not nearly filled.[60] However, Clanricarde was unsuccessful in his efforts to secure depots for either of his towns.

In the spring 1846, hundreds of local relief committees were set up throughout the country to distribute provisions to the poor at affordable prices. Their activities were jointly funded by local subscriptions and government donations. As lord lieutenant of the county, Clanricarde had responsibility for nominating relief committees but he delegated much of that work to his deputy lieutenants. When requested by the relief commission to nominate such a committee for the district comprising the baronies of Ballymoe, Killian and Tiaquin in March 1846, he replied that the district was a very great distance from his residence and he had not sufficient local knowledge to enable him to execute the desire of the commission. He recommended that it should seek the assistance of local magistrates and deputy lieutenants such as Denis Kelly of Castlekelly, Robert French of Monivea Castle and Sir Michael Bellew of Mountbellew in selecting the persons to compose the relief committee. [61]

Clanricarde took a greater interest in the relief of distress in his own district and wrote to John Pitt Kennedy, secretary of the relief commission, in March 1846, informing him of a meeting which had been held in Loughrea for the purposes of forming a relief committee and raising subscriptions. He urged Kennedy to send a supply of maize to that area to keep down the price of corn, stating that speculators had purchased large quantities of oats at Galway with a view to realising exorbitant profits as a result of the impending Famine.[62] In April he wrote to the lord lieutenant on behalf of the Loughrea committee, enclosing a memorial of 27 subscribers to a fund of £820 to supply provisions to the Loughrea poor law union. He pleaded with the government to make a proportionate contribution to the fund to which he and his wife had contributed £350. Dr Thomas Coen, Catholic bishop of Clonfert, who had chaired the meeting of magistrates, clergy, gentlemen and ratepayers, signed the memorial. The bishop stated that the memorialists required either a pecuniary contribution to their fund or a grant of Indian corn which would be cheap food for the labouring class. The population of the union was very considerable with two large market towns, Loughrea and Portumna, and several smaller ones. He contended that the people had, at all times been industrious, quiet, peaceably disposed, and deserving of the kind consideration of the government and the gentry.[63]

Ambrose O'Kelly, a local magistrate, from Gurtray, a townland situated close to Portumna, sent to the then chief secretary, Lord Lincoln, an account of the terrible distress being endured by 211 inhabitants living in five local townlands in a district of less than two miles in diameter between the post towns of Killimor, Eyrecourt and Portumna. O'Kelly urged the government to send the county inspector or sub-inspector to enquire into the distress and stated that he and two other local magistrates had taken preparatory steps to apply for public works.[64] A letter written by O'Kelly's daughter-in-law to her grandchildren in 1943 stated that during the Famine, 'people lay down to die by the roadside', in the Portumna area. O'Kelly rescued as many of them as he could, brought them to his house at Gurtray, and fed them with gruel. The letter also stated that starving unfortunates lay on mattresses in O'Kelly's kitchen while the owner and his family deprived themselves of food in order to have more to give to these starving people.[65]

By April 1846, O'Kelly had become acting chairman of a parochial relief committee in Portumna which received a donation of £50 from Clanricarde. The committee resolved that the government should match the funds collected for the purchase of Indian meal 'as otherwise the suffering must be extreme before relief from public works would be available'.[66] Clanricarde supported the committee's request by again writing to Kennedy, urging him to send Indian corn to the Portumna district. He feared that if food prices were allowed to rise in anticipation of Famine the distress would be much aggravated.[67]

In January 1847, the secretary of the Portumna relief committee, Denis Hynes, informed Routh that the poorhouse for the division at Loughrea had more inmates than it could cater for and 'is most melancholy, so much so, that no one will recommend the destitute to seek there a temporary asylum'.[68] Hynes enclosed a list of over 60 subscribers to a sum of £302. Clanricarde and other members of his family contributed £155 of that total. He donated regularly to many local relief committees, even those having no connection whatever with his estate. These donations would help to placate the starving masses and maintain relative peace and calm in his area. However, he did not actively involve himself in the work of any local relief committees, leaving that business to lesser local gentry.

Food shortages led to unrest and agitation in many parts of Ireland. Reports of disturbances were forwarded to Dublin Castle from the neighbourhood of Clanricarde's estate. In March 1846, Hobart, the police inspector for the district of Marble Hill, reported to the inspector general in Dublin that 100 people had assembled at Whitegate near the Co. Clare border to obtain food, to intimidate the farmers from the disposing of wheat out of the neighbourhood and to prevent boats from bringing off the wheat from Williamstown (a harbour on the river Shannon). Hobart highlighted the absolute distress of 200 families, their lack of means of obtaining food and the alarm that existed among those who had food of it being 'wrestled from them by force'.[69] Clanricarde's tenants would most probably have been involved in this protest as they also used that harbour to export their corn.

S.R. Pole, the captain in charge of the corn depot at the nearby town of Banagher on the eastern bank of the Shannon, addressed a similar topic when, in June 1846, he reported a potentially serious situation to Routh. Pole received information that upwards of 800 starving men had assembled within two miles of Banagher with the intention of entering that town to demand employment or food.[70] These people called on the board of works to construct a new road to connect the towns of Banagher and Portumna.[71] Since the Banagher corn depot also supplied the tenants of Clanricarde's estate it is possible that some of them took part in this protest.

While Clanricarde publicly pleaded the case for the starving masses he was also concerned for the safety of property and landowners against agrarian outrages. In a letter to the relief commission in February 1846, he drew attention to the lawlessness which existed in parts of his county. When it was proposed to hold a meeting in the barony of Ballymoe, with a view to alleviating the distress in the district, Clanricarde informed John Pitt Kennedy, that the local magistrate, Denis Kelly, had advised against it because 'the conduct of the peasantry in that neighbourhood having been of late very lawless and riotous such a meeting might appear intended as a bribe ... and do more harm than good'.[72]

In assessing the situation at local level Clanricarde showed himself to be very practical and well informed. He argued that if the outrages committed by the people deterred the government from giving assistance that it might otherwise give, then 'that fact ought to be made known in the country'. He felt that assistance should be given through food depots rather than money, due to the unrest in parts of the country.

I apprehend no speculator would dare to risk a cargo of food to be conveyed through the country in its present disordered and anarchical condition. Such a cargo would require to be strongly guarded as is true that the people are in want of their usual store of food.[73]

In February 1846, he declared in the house of lords that a great part of Ireland was already in a state of insurrection and demanded instant action by the government in the form of a bill for the protection of life and property in Ireland. That would enable the lord lieutenant to place any district under martial law by issuing a proclamation.[74] This proposal prompted a fierce attack in the house of commons by the Irish MP, William Smith O'Brien, who stated that, although famine was menacing Ireland, the government sent soldiers rather than food so that Ireland was to starve but be coerced.[75]

Clanricarde's fears concerning the security of landowners was well founded, since he himself was the subject of a death threat. An account of a plot to assassinate him was detailed in an unsigned letter sent from the parish of Killimor to Captain Burke in March 1846.[76] The author of the letter recounted how he was accosted by three intoxicated would-be assassins while out shooting plover on the banks of the Shannon. They stated that Clanricarde was to have been shot at the races but

> not having turned up there it was agreed upon his next return to Portumna to finish him as everything was arranged … and they had a friend at one of the hotels where he was to change horses to appraise them of his coming. It was settled that he should, if possible, be finished before he got into Tipperary.[77]

He alleged that Clanricarde was the enemy who brought in a law, 'the Insurrection Act' to Ireland. Clanricarde attached sufficient importance to the threat that he wrote to the leader of the Liberal party, Lord John Russell. He conveyed to Russell his fear of being he could be shot on account of speeches he had made in parliament. He claimed he had been warned by both a policeman and a peasant not to attend the Ormonde hunt races in Tipperary, which were held each year in March, not far from the town of Portumna.[78] Clanricarde was prepared to plead the case for the starving masses but was equally keen to maintain law and order to protect the lives and property of his fellow gentry by the introduction of coercive measures.

2. Cabinet minister during the Famine

Sir Robert Peel's controversial repeal of the corn laws was undertaken at great political cost to himself. The protectionist wing of his Tory party opposed its difficult passage through the houses of parliament. It led to the collapse of his government, brought down by a vote on an Irish Coercion bill, that Clanricarde, for one, had sought earlier that year. Peel had actually resigned over the corn laws issue on 5 December 1845 but Lord John Russell, the then leader of the Liberal party, was unable to form a government. During the uncertain period when it seemed, from newspapers reports, that Russell was likely to head a new administration, Clanricarde wrote to him from Portumna, on 21 December 1845, to impress upon him the importance of putting Ireland at the top of the agenda of his new government.

> And I wish to lose no time in impressing upon you that the many difficulties you have to encounter, the state of Ireland is by no means the least. In my opinion it is the most serious. It is of such importance ... that party considerations must be allowed little weight.[1]

In a typical political statement, Clanricarde laid much of the blame for the state of lawlessness in parts of Ireland squarely on the shoulders of the Tory government and he told Russell that all sensible men of property in Ireland, even those of Conservative persuasion, would support a moderate Liberal administration.[2] While he was anxious to inform Russell as to the state of Ireland, Clanricarde was also positioning himself to be included in the new cabinet. He conveyed this message more explicitly to Russell two days later when he remarked that 'there is no man with whom, or under whom, I would more willingly hold office'.[3]

Peel finally resigned on 27 June 1846 and a new Liberal administration under Lord John Russell was formed. With the accession to power of Russell, prospects looked brighter as the Liberals were generally viewed to be more sympathetic to Ireland's needs than the Tories. Russell saw his mission as completing the task of integrating Catholic Ireland into the Union and more than any other prime minister he combined the vision and the will to make the Union a workable reality.[4] He proposed to do this by giving Irish Catholics equal treatment with all other British subjects and by implementing his policy of 'justice for Ireland'.

Before referring to the policies adopted by the new government in which Clanricarde was a minister, it is necessary to understand the various economic viewpoints being advanced by Liberal supporters at that time to resolve Ireland's difficulties resulting from overpopulation and underdevelopment. One school of orthodox economic thinkers emphasised the necessity of commercial and financial reform. Its adherents believed that the reorganisation of landholding was essential to stimulate large-scale capital farming leading to greater productivity. State intervention would be required to provide public infrastructure and some assisted emigration, but they had begun to lean towards the 'promotion of agencies of social control and economic stimulation'.[5] They favoured church reform and Catholic endowment but were hostile to O'Connell's Repeal movement. Furthermore, the majority of this group of moderate Liberals were resolutely opposed to a compulsory poor law for Ireland on the grounds that 'it would drain away scarce resources from employment into useless relief of the able bodied'.[6]

Politically, this section of the party centred on the third marquis of Lansdowne, although he was one of those who supported a poor law for Ireland. It also included Lords Clanricarde and Monteagle, with Lord Palmerston also being attracted to orthodox economic ideas and gravitating to this wing of the party.[7] These men were perceived as landowners committed to maximising the productivity of their estates. Clanricarde did not live up to this image of an improving landlord and his public utterances in London on reforming agricultural practices were not put into effect on his Irish estate.

A further group of economists asserted that the root cause of Ireland's problems lay in the relationship between landlord and tenant. This group favoured an alternative system of peasant proprietorship, as existed in other European countries. They believed that the Famine presented the government with an opportunity to intervene to reconstruct Irish society.[8] Both Russell and the Irish landowner, Lord Bessborough, had leanings towards this type of interventionist reform policy. Russell's political thinking was greatly influenced by the policies promoted by Charles James Fox in the late eighteenth century. Fox was a proponent of the cultural distinctiveness of the Liberal aristocracy and of the rights and liberties of the popular masses. For this reason, the term 'Foxite' was used to describe those members of the Liberal party who subscribed to his views.

The 'Manchester school' of economic thinkers argued for free trade (*laissez faire*) and sought to put the onus for agricultural improvement on Irish landowners, whom they blamed for abdicating their responsibility in this regard. They believed that Ireland was quite a wealthy country and sought measures to make landowners provide employment for the poor. This group included Charles Wood, who became chancellor of the exchequer, and Charles Trevelyan, who acted as assistant secretary at the treasury and held sway over exchequer spending in Ireland. Both these men played significant roles in deciding Irish Famine policy. While Clanricarde did not subscribe to this group's thinking, he acknowledged the country's wealth in his letter to Freemantle in 1845 and identified one of the contributory causes of the Famine by observing that 'the country is rich and, in many respects, prosperous at this time. But the main demand for agricultural [produce] has aggravated the consequences of the disease in the potatoes by causing an unusually large and rapid export of grain, particularly of oats'.[9]

In tandem with these economic philosophies was the concept of providentialism, the idea that failure of the potato crop was a divine judgement against the Irish people. Providentialism took many forms, but when combined with the thinking of the Manchester school it provided a moralistic framework to explain to contemporaries the underlying causes of the Irish Famine. This put the blame for the catastrophe on the moral failings of Irishmen of all classes.[10] Liberals, including Trevelyan, Wood and home secretary, George Grey, embraced this form of moralism.[11] The composition of the cabinet, therefore, allowed frictions and tensions to develop, often caused by its diverse factions disagreeing over Irish Famine policy. As a result Russell was unable to exercise control over his cabinet or introduce the reforms he had envisaged for Ireland and Trevelyan was afforded unbridled freedom to pursue his economic objectives at the expense of human life in Ireland.

Successive British cabinets of the 19th century were noteworthy for the significant number of landowners included in their ranks. Russell's cabinet included three Irish landlords. Palmerston became foreign secretary, Lansdowne served as lord president of the council, while Clanricarde, despite his opposition to the introduction of a poor law system for Ireland, was given the portfolio of postmaster-general. Besssborough, a personal friend of Russell's, was given the position of lord lieutenant of Ireland until his sudden death in May 1847. In addition, a significant number of Irish Catholics were given important positions in Russell's administration. The O'Conor Don became lord of the treasury, while Richard Lalor Shiel was appointed master of the mint. Thomas Nicholas Redington, a Catholic landowner from the southern part of Co. Galway, became under-secretary at Dublin Castle and he, along with Bessborough, and later Clarendon, played an important role in the administration of Irish Famine relief.

Redington had supported a poor law for Ireland and was deemed to have been a conscientious chairman of the board of guardians of the Galway poor law union until his appointment to Dublin Castle in 1846. He represented Dundalk in the house of commons as a Liberal MP. Although a distant cousin of Clanricarde, relations between the two men were strained for it was thought that Redington had aspirations to represent Co. Galway in parliament.[12] Redington maintained a high profile in his native county and enjoyed the support of the influential Galway newspaper, the *Tuam Herald*. But if he had intentions of representing Co. Galway, he was likely to have little chance of success against the interest of Clanricarde, the wealthiest and most powerful landowner in the entire county.[13]

A constant source of division both inside and outside Russell's cabinet was the question of religious practice. Ireland's population, 81 per cent of which was Catholic, was greatly mistrusted by the British establishment, particularly that section aligned to O'Connell's Repeal movement. Some economists of that era, such as Chalmers, Sumner and Copleston, had a profound influence over a large section of the British elite and were imbued with an ethos of evangelical protestantism. These saw the blight as divine vengeance against Irish catholicism and on the British state that had recently committed such 'national sins' as endowing the Catholic seminary at Maynooth.[14] Clanricarde did not subscribe to that viewpoint and supported government policies favourable to Catholics. He was a committed emancipationist and in that regard he differed greatly from his neighbour, the earl of Clancarty, on the Garbally estate in Ballinasloe whose family's efforts at proselytising their tenantry during the Famine created great interdenominational bitterness.[15] While eager to maintain the integrity of the protestant church in Ireland, Clanricarde was willing to pay a tax for the support of the Catholic clergy, as he 'would think it a very cheap purchase of peace and an improved condition of society'.[16]

He was a constant supporter of Catholic rights and privileges even at the risk of incurring the wrath of some of his protestant colleagues. Clanricarde's tolerance, openness and non-sectarian attitude towards Catholics was well articulated in various debates in the house of lords. In one such debate in 1838, he stated that all British subjects should have equal rights and privileges as long as they displayed allegiance to the crown and he thought a declaration of faith unnecessary by any class of christians.[17] In his contribution to another debate, in 1842, on the state of Co. Tipperary, he acknowledged the influence of the Catholic clergy in maintaining law and order in Ireland.[18]

In 1844, he castigated the Tories for the manner in which they had handled Irish affairs accusing them of 'holding authority there by military occupation and by no other power whatever'.[19] Clanricarde held them responsible for the excited state of parts of Ireland and on a wider scale he criticised the government for its failure to trust Irish Catholics. He maintained that

> there existed a feeling that the Roman Catholics could not be safely entrusted with political power, or with the exercise of those full and free franchises which the rest of the country enjoyed ... that they could not admit the people of Ireland to a full, fair and free equality with the rest of the country in the exercise of the rights of the subjects of the British Empire.[20]

He was also critical of the government's banning of O'Connell's planned monster meeting at Clontarf in 1843, deeming the steps taken by the government to have been characterised by rashness and to have incurred the risk of violence. Whatever might have been said of Mr O'Connell, Clanricarde believed that 'it was owing to the immense influence of the learned gentleman, and which he exercised effectually, that the day passed off without bloodshed'.[21] Clanricarde argued that if Peel's government had addressed other Irish grievances such as land tenure and religious discrimination 'the progress of Repeal might have been retarded'.[22]

The government's attempt to suppress O'Connell's monster meetings was accompanied by the dismissal of Irish magistrates who had supported the Repeal movement. In the house of lords, Clanricarde raised the case of Lord French, a magistrate from Caltra, Co. Galway, who was dismissed because he had intimated his intention of attending a Repeal meeting. Clanricarde moved a resolution that 'such an intimation was not sufficient grounds for dismissing magistrates from the commission of the peace and that such dismissals were unconstitutional, unjust and inexpedient'.[23]

The great Catholic adversary of the successive British governments was Dr John MacHale, archbishop of Tuam. In 1847, Clanricarde wrote to Clarendon to warn him of the dangers involved in dealing with MacHale and the nationalist priests.

> About the priesthood of this country and MacHale you must be very cautious. I know the latter very well and used to talk very freely … MacHale, who is very anti-Pope and for the independence of the Hibernian Church would at all times be a slippery and dangerous friend …[24]

He suggested that the first step Russell's government ought to take was to establish diplomatic relations with the pope. 'That would be a great blow to MacHale and the turbulent priests and make us all appear good Roman Catholics'.[25] He advised Russell that it would be injudicious to touch the Hiberno-Catholic church question until relations between that church and Rome were more clearly established.[26] He also conveyed his positive impressions of the Irish landed Catholics suggesting that 'Roman catholics of wealth, intelligence and respectability to be the most loyal, monarchical and truly conservative portion of the Irish, excepting only the highest class of church of England'.[27] After the 1848 Young Ireland rising, Clanricarde felt obliged to deny the assertion made by Lord Redesdale that at least four-fifths of Irish Roman Catholics were disloyal. He maintained that 'the Roman catholic soldiers, police and constabulary were as true and loyal as any in the service of her majesty'.[28]

Russell's government had a good working relationship with Dr Murray, archbishop of Dublin, who supported the Queen's Colleges, despite MacHale's opposition to them. Clanricarde gave his blessing to these colleges and also supported the funding of Maynooth College.[29] Unlike MacHale and Redington, he supported the national school system of education, declaring that 'no better system of Christian education existed in any part of the civilised world'.[30] The appointment of Dr Cullen as archbishop of Armagh signalled the beginning of a turbulent relationship between the Catholic church and the government. Clanricarde was displeased with Cullen's orchestration, at the synod of Thurles in 1850, of a narrow majority in favour of Rome's opposition to the Queen's Colleges.[31]

When Archbishop Wiseman announced, in 1850, that the Catholic hierarchy was to be restored in England an angry Lord John Russell wrote an open letter describing the Catholic mass and sacraments as 'mummeries of superstition'.[32] Even Clanricarde could write, rather out of character, that 'if the Romans ... put their Church so forward the practices thereof will be plainly expounded'.[33]

At local level, Clanricarde worked closely with the bishop of Clonfert, Thomas Coen, in seeking government assistance to relieve Famine distress. Like many other protestant landlords, Clanricarde was also supportive of Catholics in providing land and financial assistance for the building of churches and schools for his tenants.[34] Many instances of his generosity were recorded in the local press. In January 1843, the *Tuam Herald* noted that

> it is with great pleasure we recount the following very kind and liberal acts of benevolence of the marquis of Clanricarde. His Lordship has generously given to the Revd Michael Clarke P.P. Woodford and his successors a lease of lives of 14 acres of land at a nominal rent of £2 per annum, on which there has been erected a very handsome Catholic Church and parochial house, the former for the use of a portion of his Lordship's tenantry.[35]

Clanricarde's good working relationship with the Catholic community in Co. Galway was due in part to his family's long association with that religion. His mother though committed to raising her son in the protestant religion, remained a staunch Catholic throughout her long life.[36] She made several donations to Catholic causes locally and supported the building of St Brigid's church, Portumna, in 1827.[37] Clanricarde's understanding and forbearance of Catholics was also influenced by the fact that a substantial number of the Galway gentry, on whom he depended for political support, were Catholic, as was the overwhelming majority of the tenants on his estate. This broad support would prove beneficial in the execution of his duty as lieutenant of the county, since he believed that the influence of the Catholic clergy was necessary in preventing agrarian unrest and preserving law and order amongst the peasantry. Clanricarde must be credited with holding a consistent line in his treatment of Catholics at government and local level.

Before the general election of 1847, Clanricarde attempted to initiate a detailed analysis of the Liberal party's political support in Ireland.[38] He believed that there was an opportunity to raise a powerful party 'to support the government, the crown and the Union'. He suggested that he, Redington and Bessborough should undertake that task and felt that in order to be successful it would be necessary to bestow patronage on parties not associated with the government.

> We must vary according to the varying circumstances of various districts, leaning sometimes to Repealers, sometimes to the Tories, endeavouring to conciliate all liberal, moderate men, and avoiding, as far as we can conflict with any save and except the 'Young Ireland' small party.[39]

He deemed such a conciliatory approach necessary so that the new parliament could address religious questions that would 'excite the public mind in England and Ireland'.[40] He suggested that, in carrying out this work, they should consult his uncle, Sir John Burke, since 'there is hardly a man who has more extensive acquaintance of the landed gentry of Ireland'.[41] He also urged that the views of his Peelite friend, William Gregory, who had Liberal tendencies, be sought on Irish affairs. Clanricarde placed particular emphasis on the Kildare Street Club in Dublin as a suitable place to contact many Irish landlords.

> Kildare St Club is the real place in which knowledge of every landlord's estate … of the general state of almost every constituency, and of the bias of persons of every class may be learned. Incessant gossip of local Irish, and provincial politics goes on there every day.[42]

However, Lord John Russell did not have such a high opinion of that club, cynically stating that the 'consumption of claret had been so little at Kildare Street recently that there really must be distress in Ireland'.[43] Bessborough declined to place his trust in either John Burke or William Gregory,[44] and neither he nor Redington agreed with raising a party in Ireland based solely on landlord connections and interests, so Clanricarde's plan failed to materialize.[45]

At local level, Clanricarde exerted greater political influence, and much evidence exists to highlight his ability to control the outcome of elections within the county and borough of Galway. Not only did he ensure the return of his cousin, Sir Thomas Burke, and later his own son, Lord Dunkellin, as Liberal candidates in a number of political contests but he also had an input into selecting the successful Tory candidate in the system which operated with Co. Galway's two most powerful political factions.[46] Pre-election speeches, made by opposition candidates, were designed to placate the powerful Clanricarde, 'a wealthy man and possessed of great influence'.[47] In replying to a request for electoral support from the Tory, Denis Daly, in July 1847, Clanricarde replied: 'I must give you the same reply I have already given to St

George and to Bodkin, which is that I wish to support or oppose no candidates for our county except Captain Tom ...'[48] Clanricarde was even able to persuade his Tory friend, William Gregory, into urging his tenants to vote for Sir Thomas Burke, a Liberal, rather than the Tory candidate, Robert Daly, in the county election of 1847.

In a letter to Russell in February 1847, Clanricarde outlined how, having received Redington's note begging him to send his agent to Galway to help J.H. Monahan in the forthcoming election, he immediately wrote to Sir Thomas Burke, 'the most popular man in our county', and asked him to mobilize the Clanricarde tenantry. He also sent his agent and head clerk to work on Monahan's behalf.[49] Clanricarde felt uncomfortable with his involvement in this process and encouraged Russell to say little about the matter as it might affect Monahan's chances of electoral success. 'I suppose this is very unconstitutional but I do not think it at all wrong. I gave no direction or permission to use any threats in my name.'[50] Monahan won the seat to represent Galway borough in parliament. Clanricarde proposed to Russell to appoint Monahan as Irish attorney general and he fulfilled that role until 1850.[51]

Clanricarde and his son spared no expense in securing the votes of the electors. In Galway borough elections the voters were well treated by Dunkellin's agent, who supplied the freemen with lots of whiskey. On polling day, a Clanricarde supporter stood beside each polling booth and gave a piece of paper to those who pledged to vote for Dunkellin. The voter then presented the paper at Dunkellin's committee rooms and received an undisclosed sum of money as a reward for his vote.[52]

Repealers in Galway opposed Clanricarde's exercise of his considerable political influence in the 1847 election. An article in the *Nation* newspaper, entitled 'Whig Coercion' accused the Liberal administration, and Clanricarde in particular, of gross intimidation of the Galway voters.

> The extent of the intimidation is almost incredible. The bailiffs of Lord Clanricarde and several other landlords are going about threatening the starving tenantry with immediate extermination if they do not vote for the government candidate ... the wretches on the public works have been threatened by a government officer with dismissal if they should prove refractory.[53]

The report also stated that Sir Thomas Burke had gone into Galway town and forced Lord Clanricarde's tenants to vote for Monahan against their will. However, a Repeal meeting, held in Galway, instructed the Young Ireland MP, William Smith O'Brien, to ask the prime minister whether Clanricarde had sanctioned such coercion. O'Brien also wrote to Clanricarde about the matter but received a mere formal reply, indicating the cabinet minister's indifference to O'Brien's objection.[54]

The catastrophic failure of the potato crop in 1846 shocked Lord John Russell's new administration. His focus had been directed towards his 'comprehensive reform measures for Ireland' and he had given little attention to a Famine relief programme to combat the unprecedented disaster. Clanricarde saw himself as an advisor to the government and the prime minister on Irish affairs and frequently wrote to Russell on a range of political issues pertaining to Ireland. He also communicated with key figures in the Irish administration and had much correspondence with Lord Clarendon when he assumed the role of Irish lord lieutenant on the death of Lord Bessborough. Clanricarde was aware of the great level of destitution in Ireland and much of his correspondence with leading political figures referred to the appalling state of the country. He had already alerted Russell, in December 1845, of its critical condition, remarking that it was 'the most serious difficulty the minister of the crown, whoever he may be, will have to encounter'.[55]

Clanricarde took an active part in preparing government legislation relating to Ireland. In December 1846, he informed Russell that, having spent three days in Dublin consulting with Bessborough and the chief secretary, Labouchere, on Irish issues they had commenced drafts on a range of bills. He also confirmed to the prime minister that great disappointment existed in Ireland over the government's refusal to interfere in the provision trade. 'But the common feeling throughout the country is that we ought to have depots of provisions all through the country and keep down the price of food'.[56] He noted that the government was blamed for the export of provisions from the poorer parts of the country and for its mismanagement of the 'numerous absurd works'. Clanricarde suggested that Russell should give immediate attention to a series of Famine measures such as productive public works, wasteland reclamation, fisheries, assisted emigration and the sale and transfer of property. He confided in Russell that Bessborough was not fully aware of the extent and nature of the government's difficulties and he believed that the board of works and the commissariat 'were guided more by the treasury than the wants of the country'.[57]

With the exception of drainage, Trevelyan favoured unproductive works so that Irish landowners would not benefit at taxpayers' expense. Bessborough, however, contended that landowners had a right to expect assistance in promoting productive works to improve Irish agriculture, provided they made a reasonable contribution to the cost. Clanricarde echoed this view and having consulted many of his fellow landowners in the west of Ireland stated that

> I know that in the west there was a great desire on the part of the land-
> lord to employ the people entirely upon reproductive works ... There
> are various operations quite as useful as draining to some landholders
> ... and a facility should be given for every kind of improvement.[58]

In 1846, a new Poor Employment Act was passed containing a labour rate clause which placed responsibility for payment of all government loans on local rates. Bessborough favoured a permanent labour rate law for Ireland but Clanricarde disapproved of the idea. 'I do not think I can ever be party to such a measure. I believe in my conscience that it would condemn Ireland to eternal poverty, misery and slavery.'[59] Notwithstanding the fact that, by his own admission, much of the land in the west of Ireland remained uncultivated and unsown, he objected to Redington's proposal to 'permit as payable from the rate the tillage of the land'.[60] The Poor Employment Act caused sharp divisions within cabinet. The moderates, including Clanricarde and Palmerston, strongly objected to baronial sessions being compelled to allot funds for relief works. They maintained that this was an intrusion into the powers of the landed gentry.[61]

Clanricarde explained to the prime minister, in early January 1847, that the distress caused by the scarcity of food was 'indisputably fearful and amounting to famine in several localities' and he entreated Russell to continue sanctioning gratuitous relief where 'cases so horrible may arise as to put all ordinary considerations out of place'. Clanricarde warned Russell that the misery and despair of the peasantry and the poverty and distress of landlords were increasing. 'It is indisputable that many persons in this land are dying of starvation and thousands are on the brink of it. Are we, the government, to interfere or to stand by and see them die?'[62] Clanricarde suggested to Russell, in April 1847, that Ireland would recover in a year or two from the major calamity it had suffered, if given a little help.

> Ireland wants relief from the present, desperate misery which presses upon her: and that relief ought I think to be afforded as far as possible, firstly by aid to rates and to starving districts and secondly by advances ... drawn gradually from imperial resources.[63]

In a letter to Clarendon, Clanricarde expressed his concern as to how the vast population of Ireland was to be fed without ruin to property and disorganisation of the social fabric of the country. He was appalled at the number of destitute persons for whom he saw no possible means of survival and wondered what would happen when the soup relief was ended and the poorhouses and gaols were full. He was also concerned at the level of robbery taking place in his area. He claimed that all kinds of vegetables were being stolen, as was a considerable amount of corn, which was plucked, ground and used as food. He remarked that there was a splendid grain harvest but, as in the previous year, there would not be enough potatoes to feed the people for three months, even if none were used for seed. The corn crop was needed by the landlord, farmer and tenant to meet other liabilities. He articulated his concern for the future of landowners. 'If the landlord does not insist upon his rent he must be totally ruined, as he has not received a shilling for eight months at least and the value of the produce will be seized by other creditors'.[64]

Many of Clanricarde's tenant farmers were overburdened by poor rates and he highlighted their plight to Clarendon in August 1847.

> If you come upon that class for a large amount of rates you involve them in the destruction of the lower classes. Remember that if the English government alienate from them the landed gentry of Ireland it is not a question of 'Repeal' but one more fatal.[65]

In many of the cabinet debates on proposed relief measures for Ireland Russell found himself caught up in the conflict between the moralists who would not tolerate any further exchequer relief spending and the Irish moderates who rejected any further financial burden on their properties. Palmerston contended that if the moralist agenda was pursued the landowner would be as well qualified as the cottier to demand admission to the union workhouse.[66] However, the policies of the moralistic wing of the party, espoused principally by Charles Wood and the colonial secretary, Earl Grey, ably assisted by the like-minded Trevelyan, dominated Famine relief measures. They viewed the Famine as an opportunity to change the social structure in Ireland, to compel landlords and tenantry to end overdependence on the potato, to charge relief measures to the poor law rates and to enforce obedience to moral law.[67] Wood insisted that Irish landowners should employ the people on their own estates and suggested that the time had come when the Irish proprietor must learn to depend upon himself. The lack of effective leadership within the cabinet during the Famine period allowed Trevelyan to insist on a withdrawal of state interference in the external food trade in Ireland and to bring relief works under state control. However, common ideological ground did exist between the opposing factions in their desire to remove the cottier class and commercialise Irish agriculture.

Clanricarde's membership of the cabinet reduced his contributions to house of lords debates. This may have been due to the extra workload and responsibility associated with ministerial office, cabinet confidentiality and to his determination to avoid controversy. His attitude towards the poor law mellowed considerably and in the house of lords he confessed that, while no one had been more opposed to a poor law for Ireland than he, the system had already been in operation for almost ten years, and as there were more than two million destitute people in the country, 'they must now determine to give a really efficient poor law to Ireland'.[68] He was prepared to tolerate a series of measures in an amended poor law bill of 1847 which in earlier years would have been totally unacceptable to him. He declared that for some years to come there would be a heavy burden on land and argued that the effects of the calamity in Ireland would be of a permanent nature.[69] He even insisted that proper legal regulations should be sanctioned to compel all proprietors of land in Ireland to contribute their fair share to the support of the poor.[70] His change in attitude was obviously influenced by the unprecedented scale of the disaster confronting the government and he realised that its chief priority was to curb the increasing mortality rate in Ireland.

The 1847 Amended Poor Law Act provided for the setting up of 33 additional poor law unions in Ireland. Portumna union was one of these, encompassing an area of 77,046 acres and catering for a population of 14,939 persons. Its workhouse, in Portumna town, was built and furnished at a cost of £7,875 to accommodate 600 inmates, the first of which was admitted in 1852.[71] Clanricarde became chairman of its board of guardians, further reflecting his softening attitude towards the poor law in Ireland given that, 10 years earlier as the union's largest landowner, he had not fulfilled that role for the Loughrea board of guardians.

He enthusiastically supported the 'Gregory Clause', an amendment of the 1847 Act, introduced by his friend, William Gregory. This clause stipulated that anyone owning more than a quarter acre of land could not be given relief either inside or outside the workhouse. Clanricarde was aware of the potential consequences of the 'Gregory Clause' for great numbers of destitute tenants in the west of Ireland but considered that the measure would bring about a necessary fundamental change in Irish agriculture. In a debate on the bill he stated that 'from the change going on in Ireland those who had hitherto lived by holding small pieces of ground would no longer be able to do so. ... The clause tended to make less difficult a change which must take place, and the sooner the better.'[72] Despite their difficult circumstances, a number of tenants on Clanricarde's estate refused to give up their homes to enter the workhouse. His agent, Robert D'Arcy, claimed that he knew men holding 10 acres of land in as great destitution as the person receiving outdoor relief, yet they retained their land and disentitled themselves to relief rather than part with it.[73] While the Act excluded such persons from relief, Clarendon confirmed to Clanricarde his support for the alleviation of suffering of their dependants.[74] Both Clanricarde and Lansdowne were disappointed at Clarendon's lenient interpretation of the clause but reports of impending starvation forced the cabinet to concede to Clarendon's wishes, albeit in extreme cases.[75]

By 1849, 22 poor law unions, located principally along the western seaboard, were declared bankrupt as a result of the severity of the Famine. Loughrea union was not designated as one of that group, but it was bounded by several others that were. A Rate-in-Aid bill was designed to levy all taxpayers in Ireland to support these distressed unions. Clanricarde had suggested this approach to Clarendon as early as August 1847, when he stated that 'you must soon try the collection of a low rate throughout Ireland and insist on it being rigorously levied'.[76] The government intended the bill to end the dependence of bankrupt unions on the treasury. It became law on 24

May 1849, much to the anger of landlords in the north and east of the country who were levied to support the distress in the west and south. Clanricarde represented the interests of the distressed unions by strongly disagreeing with the assertion that Ulster landlords were entitled to be exempted from paying the levy.

The measure did not find favour with many other Irish landlords, including the earl of Rosse, a Tory, from neighbouring Parsonstown in Co. Offaly, who stated that he did not believe any precedent existed for a Rate-in-Aid Act. He thought 'the mischievous consequences' of it would be to diminish employment and prevent the introduction of capital into the country. He saw no reason why the taxation should not be equalised in every part of the kingdom.[77] In responding to that suggestion in the house of lords, Clanricarde displayed a significant change of attitude in relation to taxation. He argued that Ireland had enjoyed a great exemption from taxes in comparison with Great Britain and she 'should no longer leave the charge for the relief of Irish destitution to be entirely defrayed by Great Britain'. He contended that

> it was only equitable and proper that Irish property should be called upon to contribute its fair quota to the relief of those immediately connected with it, before any further demand … be made on the already heavily taxed and industrious people of this country [England] for the special relief of Irish distress.[78]

Furthermore, in the house of lords, in 1849, Clanricarde, although connected with property in a distressed part of Ireland, protested against the notion that exorbitant rates of taxation had been the ruin of Irish landlords.

> This accumulated distress, afflicting so vast a population of that island, was caused, not by rates, but by causes of far more searching and terrible operations, by the repeated failure of the crops, the famine consequent on that failure and the awful visitations of disease with which it had pleased Providence … in one of those dispensations of its wisdom that we were not permitted to fathom, to afflict the country.[79]

This line of thinking was in direct contradiction of his earlier attitude while in opposition. He was now defending the government and had joined those who blamed providence for the Famine.

Lord Monteagle argued that a levy of 2½*d*. in the pound would be insufficient to meet the needs of distress in Ireland. In a debate on the matter, he stated that the levy could not be collected in most distressed unions, as they 'could not at once be payers and receivers'. He cited eight distressed unions in Connacht, with a population of 563,000 persons, in which £220,000 had been spent on relief in 1848. However, only £46,000 was raised in poor rates despite a stringent collection. He illustrated the degree of hopelessness by outlining an example that had been brought to his attention.

> The single cow of a gentleman, who had once been a considerable landed proprietor, was seized and sold, though it formed the sole support of his family; and when redeemed by a friend and restored to its former owner … it was seized a second time and sold for rates. The goats of the peasantry shared the same fate.[80]

Clanricarde responded by saying that there were places in which those who were liable to the rate would not be called upon to pay it, as some of them would also be recipients but as soon as they recovered the rate would be collected.[81] Despite major opposition, the government had its way and the rate-in-aid was levied in Ireland only.

During the later stages of the Famine, Clanricarde spent most of his time in London and lived at either one of his houses in Carlton Terrace or Stratton Street. On a visit to Portumna in 1850, he confessed that the distress there was worse than even he had anticipated and he made Russell aware of this fact.

> Until my coming hither I was not, and I do not think, you and my colleagues are really aware of the extent to which the west and south of Ireland has been ruined … and it is no light matter to the Empire that in a great portion of Ireland property should be annihilated.[82]

He argued that Repeal of the Union or any other political changes at national level was of little significance to those who were almost totally destitute and on the brink of starvation. He went on to say that it was immaterial to landowners residing in the west of Ireland to which jurisdiction they belonged.

> It is of no consequence to a Connacht man … whether there be a Repeal of the union or a separation of Ireland from England, or annexation to America or France. No change can make his financial condition worse. And that two or three million people should be in that state must be a serious consideration.[83]

While he continued to highlight the ongoing decimation of all classes in the west of Ireland, Clanricarde failed to convince his cabinet colleagues to put meaningful relief measures in place. He did not undertake any scheme of work on his own estate that involved any cost to himself and so destitution and starvation was allowed to continue there.

Inextricably linked to the causes of the Great Famine were the questions of land tenure and the relationship between landlord and tenant in Ireland.

Clanricarde's substantial correspondence with other political figures and his contributions to many political debates bear testimony to the importance he attached to these matters.

Realising that the land question was at the root of much agrarian unrest in Ireland, Peel's government had established the Devon commission, in 1843, to examine the problems associated with land tenure. Clanricarde attacked its terms of reference, describing them as 'the most mischievous and pitiable contrivances to which a perplexed ministry ever had recourse'. He considered them to be 'a sweeping condemnation of the conduct of landlords in Ireland' and an attempt to 'effect a total alteration in the law and principle of real property'.[84] In a house of lords debate, he stated that the appointment of the commission had heightened the expectation of fixity of tenure, a reduction of rents and the curbing of the 'grasping conduct of landlords'.[85]

Lord Stanley's Compensation bill of 1845, proposed the granting of compensation to dispossessed tenants for improvements carried out on their holdings during their tenancy. Clanricarde was one of nineteen peers who signed a protest against the bill on the grounds that it contravened the law of contract. He questioned whether a tenant who had been ejected for non-payment of rent would be entitled to compensation. He used the opportunity in a subsequent house of lords debate to arouse fears amongst English and Scottish landlords that the same measure might also be introduced in Britain.[86] Both Clanricarde and Clarendon suggested, as part of the drive to eliminate middlemen, that the power of distraint should be removed from them. However, Clanricarde advised Russell in March 1847, that it would be unwise to touch the general right of landlords to distrain as the machinery necessary to implement the measure was not yet in place and tenants would withhold their rents.[87]

In contrast to Bessborough, his predecessor, Clarendon showed coolness towards Repealers and this was reflected in his comment to Clanricarde that 'they should be made to feel their nothingness'.[88] Agitation for land reform and tenant rights focused attention on landlord-tenant relations as tenant associations sprang up in some localities in Ireland during 1847.[89] While no such association was established in east Galway at that time, Clanricarde feared an upsurge in agrarian unrest, and in a letter to Clarendon, he stated that 'it is the landlord and not the tenant that required further protection'.[90]

In September 1847, he informed Clarendon of the 'considerable alarm and excitement' existing in Ireland over the 'tenant right' issue, and suggested that, in the new session of parliament, the government should propose some amendment in the laws that governed dealings between landlords and their tenants. He believed that the government should proceed cautiously as the matter was fraught with difficulties and he was concerned about some newspaper articles and a speech made by the Irish chief secretary, William Somerville, appearing to endorse 'tenant right' as government policy. He also wanted to convince Clarendon that, as a landowner from the west of Ireland, he was better informed than most about the situation in rural parts of the country.

> I do not fear that Redington or Somerville are imbued with perilous theories or opinions but I believe that a good many of the cleverest men about the Castle know little of rural life in Ireland … or I doubt if they have deep respect for the security of real property which is the basis of the entire British political, social and legal constitution.[91]

He insisted that the law must uphold the power of the landlord and the rights of property.

> All of the best statesmen of our country have constantly upheld the security, almost sacredness, of landed estates. Landed property with all its privileges belonging to it, is the aim and object of every man, of every profession, trade and calling in the United Kingdom.[92]

He encouraged Somerville not to allow any principle of land ownership to be introduced for Ireland unless it had already been applied to England and in accordance with British law.

> 'Tenant right' should not be supposed, upon any grounds, to receive any favour from anyone connected with the government unless it is founded on the common law of Great Britain and, therefore, in accordance with the rights of property and justice.[93]

Clanricarde was aware of the sentiments expressed by the agrarian radical and Young Irelander, James Fintan Lalor, at a meeting in Holycross, Co. Tipperary, in September 1847 that cottiers be given employment rather than tenancies. Clanricarde agreed with Lalor and maintained that granting leases to cottiers would put an end to improvement of estates. He enquired of Clarendon if legislation on 'fixity of tenure', 'tenant right' or 'compensation to tenants' should apply to the cottier and the squatter.[94]

Clanricarde outlined the options open to government in framing legislation, given the innumerable difficulties in trying to have compulsory enactments between landlord and tenant. He saw the necessity for legal reform to define the contractual duties of each party and to facilitate their enforcement.

> I think we may legislate in either of two ways, possibly both. We may pass an Act which shall contain a form of voluntary agreement to be entered into by landlord and tenant, giving a cheap and summary mode

of redress if it be infringed. Or we may define certain rights to belong after a certain day to tenants-at-will which they may easily enforce against an oppressive landlord, giving, in the same Act, a summary and cheap mode of enforcing his rights to the landlord.[95]

He also stated that it was not desirable that the government should do anything that 'might set one class of the community against another'.[96] Clarendon was in broad agreement with Clanricarde's proposals but added that compensation should be given for any improvements undertaken by the tenants. This suggestion was not acceptable to the Irish property-owning cabinet ministers.

One measure that Russell's government did manage to enact in order to restructure land ownership, facilitate land sales and inject fresh energy and capital into Ireland, was the Encumbered Estates Act of 1849. Clanricarde had already suggested such an approach in his letter to Russell in December 1846 in which he sought an amendment of the law to facilitate the sale and transfer of property.[97] However he objected to the proposal of Trevelyan and Jonathan Pim[98] to break up large estates into smaller lots. He communicated this objection to Russell in 1847 arguing that

> the worst estates, in every sense of the term, those on which the land labour and capital are employed and upon which the most intense wretchedness and hopelessly complicated tenures, of every kind are to be found are the small estates. The best estates in Ireland are the larger ones.[99]

In expressing this point of view, Clanricarde was attempting to ensure that his own Galway estate and those of his fellow landowners were not divided up. He feared that such a move would undermine his own powerful position and the dominant position of the landed class in Ireland. He did not contribute to the debate on the Encumbered Estates bill in the house of lords, but he later expressed his satisfaction that the measure had been of the greatest benefit to the country.[100]

Despite the great demand for reform of the land tenure system in Ireland Russell's government failed to introduce the bill it had drafted in 1851 for that purpose. The divisions within cabinet combined with Irish landlord intransigence ensured that no reform of the land tenure system in Ireland took place during the term of office of Russell's administration. The land question resurfaced to confront legislators and landowners in the 1880s when the Clanricarde estate became a symbol of landlord oppression. The resolution of the land tenure problem eventually led to the demise of Irish landlordism.

3. Clanricarde's estate and the Famine

Unlike many of his contemporaries, Clanricarde spent a significant portion of time each year on his Irish estate in Co. Galway. Even while attending to his political duties in London he made several visits to Portumna prior to, and during, the early years of the Famine. During that time much of his correspondence with key political figures was written from there. Nonetheless, in fulfilling his role as ambassador to Russia and later as a cabinet minister, he was, of necessity, away from his estate for considerable periods of each year.

Clanricarde was inattentive to his domestic affairs and took little interest in the day-to-day management of his estate. Following the accidental burning of his mansion in 1826, his seat in Portumna consisted of the steward's quarters, fitted out as a temporary dwelling. This remained his principal Irish residence for the remainder of his life, hardly befitting a man of such wealth. His new mansion in Portumna was still under construction at the time of his death in 1874 and it had not been fully completed when it was burned down in 1922. Clanricarde's preference for politics was possibly due to the fact that he inherited the estate as a minor and was not given an opportunity to gain a practical knowledge of estate management since agents carried out this work on his behalf. The most notable of these was Robert D'Arcy who acted as his agent for over thirty years.

D'Arcy lived at Woodville near Loughrea and was a substantial landowner in his own right, farming more than 1,600 acres.[1] In 1828, he succeeded J.J. Bricknell as Clanricarde's agent and continued in that position until his death in 1860 at the age of eighty years.[2] He had overall responsibility for the management of Clanricarde's property and was given considerable latitude in deciding and implementing estate policy.[3] Given that he was agent for such a long period it is obvious that D'Arcy was successful in collecting Clanricarde's rents and that was sufficient to satisfy the landlord. However, during his tenure of the agency, a deterioration in the relationship between himself and Clanricarde's tenants took place, especially in the Loughrea area, and several threats were made on his life.[4] D'Arcy compared most unfavourably with his predecessor as noted by the *Tuam Herald* in 1839.

> Mr D'Arcy, … unfortunately for the town of Loughrea, was not guided by the example of the excellent and humane gentleman, J.J. Bicknell [*sic*] esq. whom he succeeded in the agency of the Clanricarde estate and under whose management the tenantry were happy and prosperous.[5]

The local press often criticized Clanricarde for the mismanagement of his estate and for his agent's neglect of its tenants. Clanricarde was also rebuked for his failure to halt the decline of the town of Loughrea. From the evidence presented to the Devon commission in Loughrea, in 1844, and other contemporary accounts of Loughrea, it is evident that policies publicly advocated by Clanricarde at national level were not being pursued on his estate. Several of the witnesses reiterated the criticisms already levelled at the landlord and his agent.[6] Reference was made to the fact that most occupiers of land were tenants-at-will and the practice of subletting was quite extensive on the estate. It was alleged that very little fertilizer, other than seaweed, was used and that the burning of land still continued.[7] This primitive agricultural practice tended to be carried out on poor quality land or badly managed estates.

The Revd John Macklin, a parish priest in Carabane, a parish adjoining the Clanricarde estate, gave the most damning evidence against D'Arcy's land letting arrangements. Macklin confirmed that competition for land was deliberately created 'by persons sent out by the agent to secure that competition between tenants by unlawful means' and that 'the party who will be declared the tenant … has to pay a certain fine'. He gave an account of a tenant who had asked him to intercede on his behalf with Clanricarde's agent. The tenant offered the priest £50 to be passed on to D'Arcy as a bribe to secure a lease of a holding. He informed Macklin that this was common practice among prospective tenants, and the parish priest believed that it took place without Clanricarde's knowledge. At a public meeting in Loughrea, attended by many of the local gentry, Macklin outlined the grievances associated with this practice and the meeting echoed his views on the matter.

> This meeting has heard with deep regret that a great impediment has been thrown in the way of improvement in the town of Loughrea and in various parts of the estate of the marquis of Clanricarde, in consequence of the unusual, cruel and unprecedented terms attaching to the letting of lands and tenements by invariably large sums of money … to be paid by his Lordship's tenants before possession is given, and in many instances so heavy and oppressive as to entail ruin on the parties so obliged to pay and consequently become paupers.[8]

Macklin informed the Devon commission that he had brought the matter to the attention of Clanricarde who in turn had ordered an investigation.[9] D'Arcy sought to convince Clanricarde, who was then in St Petersburg, that it was a mob meeting and that he should pay no attention to it.[10] Clanricarde seems to have taken his agent's advice as no corrective action was taken and the landlord continued to ignore the many complaints concerning his agent's shoddy practices.

It is interesting that Clanricarde's agent should have given extensive evidence to the Devon commission, given his employer's misgivings as to its purpose. D'Arcy was keen to counter any evidence which might be presented by others attempting to undermine himself or the landlord. He confirmed to the commission that some people held land by lease while others were tenants-at-will and that it was Clanricarde's policy to relet land only to the best tenants. He admitted that subletting did take place but a clause against it was normally inserted into leases. He stated that Clanricarde had drained fifty or sixty acres in the neighbourhood of Portumna as an example to his tenants, and had allowed improving tenants free rent for a year or two. D'Arcy also contended that it was Clanricarde's policy to give house-building materials to improving tenants, but the extent of this practice seems to have been quite limited on the estate and was not alluded to by other witnesses.[11] In this regard Clanricarde compared unfavourably with his neighbouring landlords, Clancarty, Clonbrock, Dunsandle and Gregory who had carried out major improvements of their estates.[12]

The contemporary reports of many travellers and local reporters referring to the dilapidated state of the town of Loughrea provide further evidence of Clanricarde's lack of interest in local affairs. D'Arcy's term as Clanricarde's estate agent coincided with town's decline in prosperity, and in 1838, F.S. Bourke, in travelling through the west of Ireland, noted that

> Loughrea is a very old town and towns in general are amongst the few things which improve with age but Loughrea is a most ugly exception. The marquis of Clanricarde is the principal proprietor of this place and of the surrounding land. He seems to take little or no interest in the improvement of his estates.[13]

The *Tuam Herald*, in writing on the same topic, remarked that 'much rests with the proprietor of Loughrea to do, to ameliorate the condition of his subjects and tenants'. It cited 'the disturbed state of the baronies of Leitrim and Longford as a cause for the absence of capital investment which reduced the town of Loughrea to ruin'.[14] A number of the witnesses to the Devon commission also cited the lack of employment and capital as a reason for so much destitution and poverty on Clanricarde's estate and in its largest town.[15] The poor state of the town was later confirmed by a reference in the *Parliamentary Gazetteer of Ireland*.

> Yet, in spite of its extent, its bustle, and its somewhat urban aspect, it totally fails to relieve the town from a prevailing character of dinginess, dirtiness and neglect ... the general edificing is poor and slovenly; the outskirts are squalid and putrefying; and the predominant physique is filth, disturbed and made extra noticeable and insufferably odious by awakening activity.[16]

The newly appointed vice-guardians of the Loughrea union added their voice of condemnation of the appalling state of the town and its hinterland in their report to the poor law commissioners in 1848. 'The extreme filth of the dwellings of the poor in the lanes and passages of this town and of its many villages throughout the union is most disgraceful and calls for improvement'.[17] The guardians stated that they were willing to supply lime, free of charge, to the poor, to whitewash their cabins if given any encouragement by 'the respectable residents of the town'.[18]

Clanricarde's lack of interest in his domestic affairs did not go unnoticed at the highest level of the Irish administration. His frequent accounts to government concerning the deplorable distress in Co. Galway led a frustrated Clarendon to make reference to 'Clanricarde's wretchedly managed estate at Portumna' in correspondence with Russell in 1849.[19] This comment indicated the gulf that existed between Clanricarde's public image as that of an improving landlord and how he was perceived by some of his peers.

Clanricarde was equally negligent in ensuring the implementation of government policies locally to cater for an impoverished tenantry. In a letter to Russell, he confirmed his support for the inclusion of a permanent out-door relief measure for the destitute and infirm in the Poor Law Amendment Act of 1847. 'I agree that out-door relief may be conceded to the infirm, and even the right to such relief may be conceded if "infirmity" be defined, and the poor-house "test" retained when guardians choose to require it.'[20] However, he had a particular difficulty with the clause in the Act which required poor law guardians to appoint relieving officers. This measure, more than any other, set him against the poor law commissioners as he attempted to resist any extra burden of rates on himself or local landowners. In a house of lords debate in 1847, he stated that only such relieving officers as were deemed necessary would be appointed and it should not be necessary to appoint officers to all unions.[21]

He obviously did not envisage such officers being appointed in the Loughrea union as he wrote to Redington, in August 1847, complaining that the Loughrea board of guardians had been requested by the poor law commissioners to appoint a half dozen relieving officers 'at absurd salaries'. He stated that to make such appointments would be 'monstrous' and he did not intend to cooperate with the scheme. 'For myself I can only say I will be no party in any capacity to such a proceeding and I hope the entire board of my union will say the same.'[22] He accused the commissioners of being 'utterly ignorant of the state of unions, paupers and guardians' and he pleaded with Clarendon to 'make the poor law commissioners enforce sound economical views of out-door relief in the different unions'.[23] He also wrote to Somerville informing him that the commissioners were 'rushing into a contest with boards of guardians upon … the appointment of highly salaried and totally useless relieving officers'. He believed that this policy would stir resistance to the payment of the poor rates.[24] He further maintained that relief given through local committees would be less expensive and much more efficient. Somerville defended the commissioner's actions, stating that they were merely enforcing the terms of the statute.[25]

During 1847, 920 inmates died in Loughrea workhouse and in December, a local man, John Burke, was found dead in the woods of Marble Hill. Some grains of corn were discovered in his tobacco box along with a note seeking admission to the workhouse. The poor law commissioners stated that his death might have been prevented had relieving officers been appointed by the Loughrea board of guardians. The failure to do so was obviously an attempt to economise the funds of the union in order to keep down the poor rates. That course of action was pursued with the approval of Clanricarde who was closely linked to the Loughrea board through its chairman, Sir Thomas Burke MP. By February 1848, a further 210 people had died in the workhouse and the Loughrea board of guardians had still not provided any out-door relief. This brought the board into serious conflict with the poor law commissioners. A damning report on 3 February 1848, by Dr Phelan, a poor law inspector, into the appalling conditions in the workhouse led to the board's formal dissolution and the appointment of paid vice-guardians to administer the union's affairs.[26]

In communicating his general dissatisfaction to Lord John Russell over the appointments of vice-guardians Clanricarde was particularly critical of the commissioners' attitude towards former boards of guardians.

> No attempt seems to be made by the poor law commissioners to conciliate the judgement or the feelings of those who have hitherto administered the law or who have the greatest interest in proper distribution of funds supplied to them. I know of gross cases of bad and improper, if not illegal management by paid guardians and I am told of many more.[27]

The vice-guardians, on assuming responsibility in Loughrea, reported to the poor law commissioners on the appalling state of the union and its gross neglect by the former guardians. On their first visit to the workhouse they could scarcely describe the lack of order or decency in every department. The probation wards were in a most terrible state, wet and filthy, and conducive to the spread of disease. A heap of dirty straw was piled up in one corner and several panes of glass were broken in the windows. The Indian meal stirabout fed to the inmates was thin, much burned and infamously cooked, while the milk supplied to the workhouse was more than half water. Many of the paupers were served with sour porter or beer, instead of milk, to take with their porridge. The kitchen boilers were in a disgraceful state of rust and totally unfit for culinary purposes. The water pumps were all out of order and the pipes broken or destroyed. Female paupers, who carried the water required by the workhouse from the nearby lake in buckets, were almost in a state of nudity. The women in the day rooms crouched together in masses to keep each other warm. The floors of the dormitories were disfigured and rotting from urinal and other discharges. The workhouse sewers were out of order and the cesspools had never been completed.

> We found two large heaps of manure and a quantity of other putrid substance were accumulated in these cesspools...obstructing the passage of the sewers, causing an overflow sometimes so considerable as to run over the day rooms, landing and passages and diffusing the most noxious vapours and the deadliest stench through the entire house.[28]

The vice-guardians deemed the place used as a burial ground most unsuitable. It adjoined the workhouse on a layer of hard rock so that graves could not be dug to a sufficient depth.

> When we came here we found the deceased paupers deposited in shallow pits in a part of the ground most contiguous to the fever sheds ... the dead were lying in their graves within a few feet of the heads of the living . ... We apprehend that when the heat of the summer shall arrive disease in the most deadly and concentrated form will develop.[29]

The accounting procedures for the union left much to be desired and the poor rates had not been properly collected. When the vice-guardians moved to address the problem they received little co-operation from those proprietors liable for such rates. 'We believe our directions on this head have caused no small degree of annoyance and excitement amongst the particular class to which they refer.'[30]

In a further report to the commissioners in March 1848, the vice-guardians alluded to the lack of co-operation afforded them by the members of the dissolved board who were highly indignant at their dismissal. The board's chairman, Sir Thomas Burke, wrote to the commissioners complaining that the conditions in the workhouse had disimproved and that the number of inmates had actually increased since the vice-guardians had been appointed. These allegations led to a detailed sworn inquiry which was conducted by Mr Owen Lloyd, a poor law inspector. The evidence gathered by Lloyd from witnesses well acquainted with the Loughrea union and its workhouse painted a picture of the appalling conditions existing there during the term of control of the former board.

The medical officer of the union, Henry Cloran, stated that there were 267 inmates in the hospital and sheds, built to cater for 150 persons, when the late guardians ceased to conduct the affairs of the union.[31] Dr Phelan told the inquiry that the infirmary was overcrowded with chronic and dysenteric patients, while the high mortality rate was due to the fact that many of those admitted to the workhouse were already in broken health or affected by contagious diseases.[32] Both men acknowledged the vast improvement that had occurred in the workhouse since the appointment of the vice-guardians, as did the Revd Joseph O'Loughlin, the workhouse chaplain.

In his submission to the inquiry on 30 May 1848, the Revd Thomas Burke, parish priest of Lickmolassy in the electoral division of Portumna, warned that in the event of people being unemployed during the summer months the destitution would be such that no poor law could meet. He believed that the clothing of the people was so bad as to confine them to their homes. In the town of Portumna, he and the resident magistrate, Mr Ryan, had established a woollen factory in an effort to relieve the distress. 475 individuals from 110 families were employed there. However, due to lack of demand, the number employed had been considerably reduced, and these people were then thrown on the poor rates.[33] There is no record of any such remedial initiative being undertaken by Clanricarde although he informed Clarendon, in 1847, that he had been 'busy reducing relief lists'.[34]

Coen's successor as bishop of Clonfert, Dr John Derry, drew attention to the progressive increase in the level of destitution within the union and to the ineptitude and inefficiency of the poor law system in general. He maintained that the system was at variance with sound policy, justice and morality. He disagreed with the composition of boards of guardians, 'so constituted, that its members have … a direct and pecuniary interest in keeping the poor rate at the lowest possible figure'.[35] He conceded that many of the Loughrea guardians were men of honour and humanity, committed to the service of the poor, but he also felt bound to add that, 'whatever may have been the cause, or on whatever members of that board the blame must rest, timely arrangements were not made for the relief of the poor of the union'.[36] He complained of the low moral standards in the workhouses and the risk of inmates, especially females, being corrupted. This had caused 'many a child to be kept at home in nakedness and hunger until its health and strength had been utterly destroyed'. Derry went to state that he had 'often hesitated as to the choice a starving female should make between the consequences of starvation at home and the proximate danger of moral corruption in a workhouse'.[37]

These various accounts give some insight into the conditions which existed in a union whose dominant figure was one of the wealthiest and most influential landowners in Ireland and a senior political figure in the British Empire. It is inconceivable that Clanricarde was unaware of the appalling state of Loughrea union and its workhouse, yet he made no effort to ameliorate conditions there. He publicly acknowledged the necessity for relieving officers but he was critical of the poor law commissioners when they actually appointed them. He continued to object to the appointment of vice-guardians despite the reported improvements brought about by them in his own union of

Loughrea. In 1850, he warned Russell of a deputation of Irish members seeking to meet the prime minister in order to repeal the Act which allowed outdoor relief and to abolish the power of vice-guardians to levy rates.[38] In supporting the deputation Clanricarde was protecting those landlords who did not wish to accept responsibility for the relief of destitution of their tenantry.

One of the most significant consequences of the Famine was the huge number of evictions which took place in Ireland, with up to a half a million people being displaced from their holdings during the years 1846–53.[39] The number of emigrants leaving Ireland also increased reaching a high in 1847 of 215,444.[40]

The Poor Law Act of 1838 and the amending Act of 1843 provided that either the board of guardians or ratepayers of a poor law union could authorise the expenditure of local rates on assisting the emigration of the poor. This provision was little used since the Act stipulated that in order to qualify pauper emigrants must first be inmates of a workhouse for at least three months. The anti-poor law agitation of 1842–3 led to the passing of an Act which made landlords liable for poor rates on holdings valued at under £4. This measure provided landlords with an incentive to clear small tenant farmers and cottiers from their estates. The Devon commission recognised farm consolidation through clearances, subsidised emigration and wasteland reclamation as an economic necessity. Although a select committee investigating the operation of the poor law in 1846, recommended state assisted emigration to relieve destitution in distressed districts, the government adopted the policy of minimum intervention.[41]

Prior to the Famine single evictions usually occurred, whereas during the period 1846–52 mass clearances became the norm. Pre-Famine evictions were generally undertaken for the recovery of rents, with tenants being readmitted to their holdings on payment of outstanding arrears. There were several reasons for wholesale clearances during the Famine but the landlord's principal objective was to rid his estate of poorer tenants. Some of these had become so impoverished that they had little prospect of repaying their rent arrears. In some instances landlords decided to cut their losses and eject defaulting tenants. A small number of landlords viewed private assisted emigration as a long-term economic investment to reduce the permanent burden of poor rates. Such were the difficult financial circumstances of others that they were placed 'under the necessity of ejecting or being ejected'.[42] The desire of improving landlords to modernise Irish agriculture by consolidating tiny holdings into larger more productive units necessitated land clearances. It was the belief of the Liberal administration during the Famine years, that the removal of cottiers would lead to the transformation of Ireland from a subsistence to a wage-earning economy. The Famine provided the opportunity to achieve this goal.

As early as 1839, Clanricarde had recognised the need for consolidation of holdings on his own estate. Various schemes were promoted, without resorting to evictions, to encourage tenants to emigrate. In October 1839, a meeting was convened in Loughrea to outline to the public, the poor law guardians and landed proprietors of the locality the advantages of the system of emigration operated by the Australian colonization commissioners. Clanricarde was represented at the meeting by his mother who subscribed £100 to a fund for assisting emigration from the locality to the Australian colonies. Her brother, Sir John Burke from Marble Hill, pledged £200 to the same fund.[43]

In outlining the policies then being adopted to consolidate holdings on Clanricarde's property Robert D'Arcy admitted to the Devon commission that ejectment was the method used to recover rents from defaulting tenants.[44] He explained that when land, held in partnership, became available the estate surveyor, Mr Cooper, was requested to lay it out in 15 or 20-acre holdings. D'Arcy then explained in one instance how the dispossessed persons were dealt with.

> In the harvest of 1841, I collected them [the tenants] together and said, 'you cannot live here':…and I agreed to give a free passage to America, which amounted, for forty-nine persons, to £78 18s. 4d, which was paid to the ship owner, …In the harvest of 1842, we paid for fifty-six persons, £117 18s. 9d. Lord Clanricarde paid the tenants going out in 1841, £142 6s. 2d.[45]

James Hardman Burke, a local magistrate and landowner, also confirmed that Lord Clanricarde had freighted vessels and paid the emigration fares for his tenants.[46]

Martin Cahalon, a former Clanricarde tenant, gave evidence to the commissioners concerning his eviction from a holding of a couple of acres in Loughrea, having been 29 years in occupation.[47] The Revd John Macklin explained that many tenants were evicted in his neighbourhood in the change from tillage to pasture. He stated that the creatures had come into Loughrea and got into any hut they could and some had even 'gone upon the bogs'.[48]

A letter to the *Daily Star*, in 1847, from Mr Doolan, a member of the Portumna relief committee, denied all knowledge of an allegation by a correspondent to the paper that he had seen 'a boatload of persons embarking at Portumna for Liverpool with means furnished for their voyage by the Portumna relief committee, and that they were paupers from the estate of the marquis of Clanricarde …'[49]

It is clear from the above evidence that policies of eviction and assisted emigration were being implemented on the Clanricarde estate in the early 1840s. Clanricarde remained committed to these policies throughout the

Famine years, and in a letter in December 1846, he urged the prime minister to consider assisted emigration as a useful relieving measure.

> I do beg and trust that you will have your mind sufficiently made up to announce something … upon emigration when the session opens. Every man, without a single exception, with whom I have spoken upon improvement of the country has mentioned emigration as more or less desirable or necessary and my experience, as well as observation, convinces me that you cannot effectually and promptly deal with the dense population of rural villages without recourse to it.[50]

He believed that cottiers would emigrate if given the means to do so and their land could then be given to farmers capable of cultivating it. He suggested that ships bringing timber from America should be used on their return journeys to convey emigrants to the colonies, and provisions should be made available to such emigrants. 'I am sure that £300,000 or £400,000, laid out in promoting emigration would have more effect than half a million of money expended in any other way.'[51] Despite the obvious merit in Clanricarde's proposal, an opportunity was lost by the government to alleviate congestion and distress from many parts of the west and south of Ireland.

Although he had overall responsibility for the maintenance of law and order in Co. Galway, Clanricarde took a lenient approach to evictions taking place in the county during the Famine. These evictions commanded considerable discussion time in both houses of parliament. In March 1846, Lord Londonderry alluded to newspaper reports of widespread evictions in Co. Galway and cited the eviction of seventy six families, amounting to 300 individuals, from the estate of Mr and Mrs Gerrard at Ballinlass, in the east of the county. Londonderry was scathing in his attack on the eviction of these tenants who had been prepared to pay their rents each year and who 'not only had been turned out of their houses but had even … been mercilessly driven from the ditches to which they had betaken themselves for shelter'.[52] He also argued that evictions carried out in that manner greatly contributed to the breakdown of law and order.

> If such scenes as these occurred in the south and west … was it to be wondered at, however it might be deplored, that deeds of outrage and violence should occasionally be attempted and that the law was not respected as it ought to be?[53]

Clanricarde responded tamely by stating that since he believed the facts of the case as reported to be true 'it appeared to him a proper case for inquiry and one illustrating the necessity for a change in the law of landlord and tenant'.[54] Christopher St George, a landowner from Oranmore, with an estate of almost

27,000 acres, was a Tory MP for Co. Galway (1847–52).[55] He evicted 600 tenants from his Connemara estate in west Galway in December 1847. A report resulting from a government investigation into these evictions contributed to his political ruin.[56] Although St. George was his political opponent, the report did not elicit any criticism by Clanricarde.

Another large-scale Galway eviction took place in April 1848, on the estate of Mr Blake in Tully, fifteen miles west of Galway town. An inquiry into these evictions by a poor law commissioner deemed them to be 'illegal, cruel and the cause of many deaths'.[57] It prompted the *Illustrated London News* to comment that 'justice demanded that a Bill should be passed to protect defenceless tenants from the murderous clearances of tyrannical landlords'.[58] Clanricarde clearly sided with the landlord when the matter was raised in a house of lords debate in 1848. In alluding to the Blake evictions he 'exculpated that gentleman from the proceedings which had taken place on his property, as they had been carried out without his knowledge, and had been put a stop to as soon as he became acquainted with them'.[59]

The Blake clearances drew a scathing rebuke from Archbishop John MacHale who declared that instead of hearing loud 'denunciations of oppression ... the people received only the chilling assurance that in those deaths, however numerous, there was nothing illegal or unconstitutional ... done in vindicating the rights of property'.[60] Bishop Derry, also, drew attention to the evictions taking place in the Loughrea union when, in 1848, he stated that 'in travelling through some of the electoral divisions I have seen unmistakable evidence of increased destitution, in the roofless houses from which the inmates have been cast forth to beg and die'.[61] The divisions in cabinet on the issue were evident when Lord John Russell suggested that the murders of poor cottier tenants were too horrible to bear and argued that 'if they put down assassins they should also put down the lynch law of the landlord'.[62]

In 1847, evictions on the estate of Major Denis Mahon at Strokestown, Co. Roscommon, attracted much public and media attention. Mahon had attempted to clear his estate of tenants by offering them a passage to Canada, but 3,000 of those who refused to go were evicted. He was shot dead on 2 November 1847.[63] When Clarendon sought a Special Powers Act to eliminate such assassinations Russell replied sharply stating that

> it is quite true that landlords in England would not like to be shot down like hares or partridges. But neither does any landlord in England turn out fifty persons at once, and burn their houses over their heads, giving them no provision for the future. The murders are atrocious, so are the ejectments.[64]

Palmerston, the foreign secretary, assisted the emigration of about 2,000 tenants from his Sligo estate amid a storm of protest in July 1847. Nine vessels left Sligo and the remainder sailed from Liverpool to Saint John, New Brunswick, Canada. In December 1847, Mr Adam Ferrie, a member of the legislative council of Canada, wrote an open letter on landlord emigration, naming Palmerston and Mahon for 'the hordes of half naked starving paupers … including aged infirm beggars and vagrants' who had been shipped from their estates. However, the emigration from the Palmerston estate was deemed a success since, by 1849, the number of those receiving relief had dropped to just two percent of the 1847 figure.[65]

Between December 1850 and February 1854, another of Clanricarde's fellow-cabinet ministers, Lord Lansdowne, cleared 3,900 paupers from his 60,000-acre Kenmare estate through the much-publicised efforts of his agent, W.S. Trench. As a result of these displacements, the annual poor rate of £1,500 liable on the estate was greatly reduced, thus ensuring its return to profitability.[66] The Lansdowne clearances differed from those earlier described in that they were perceived to be of a voluntary nature.

The British media vilified Irish landlords for dumping their evicted tenants at English ports and cities to be supported by the English poor law system. *The Times* declared that 'no argument that pen ever writ or heart ever indicted can match the spectacle of England positively invaded, overrun, devoured, infested, poisoned and desolated by Irish pauperism'.[67] The newspaper described Irish landlords as 'those shameless and importunate mendicants … the spoilt pets of the state'.[68] The *Illustrated London News* believed that, because of their indebtedness, Irish landowners were obliged 'to screw and extort the utmost farthing that can be got in any possible way from anybody'.[69] It declared that the cruel evictions, perpetrated by Irish landlords, had hardened Englishmen against those who, for centuries, had held the fate of Ireland in their hands.[70]

British politicians also engaged in the process of condemning Irish landlords for their negligence. Lord Brougham, in presenting a petition from the inhabitants of Liverpool, complained that, in fourteen days, 11,104 paupers had come over from Ireland to that port.[71] He contended that the landlords and priests of Ireland had furnished money for their passage.[72] Joseph Arthur Roebuck, MP for Bath, proclaimed that he had no sympathy whatever for Irish landlords, describing them as 'beggars'.[73] Another MP, Archibald Hastie, described Irish landlords as men who 'had done nothing but sit down and howl for English money'.[74] Clanricarde's response to the onslaught was quite muted. In a debate on Irish emigration he observed that 'the benevolence of England had been excessive, and, in many cases money had been sent to individuals in Ireland to be laid out at their own discretion'.[75] He did, however, remind the English that, in more prosperous times, cheap Irish labour had been of great benefit in building up the great towns of England.[76] In writing to Somerville in 1847, he highlighted the extreme unpopularity of Irish landlords with the British public. 'I am sorry to say there is a feeling of

exasperation in this country against Irishmen and especially Irish landlords ...
the state of things in London is terrible and the pressure has set us upon the
English landlords who are in debt.'[77]

This anti-Irish feeling made it easier for Russell's government to amend
the Irish poor law in June 1847 so that Irish landlords were obliged to support
the Irish paupers through poor rates. The 'Gregory Clause' allowed Irish
landowners legally evict defaulting tenants and protect themselves from
possible ruin. This piece of legislation, more than any other government
measure, altered the demographic landscape of much of the west and south of
Ireland as thousands of cottiers were displaced from their holdings. In 1846,
over 3,500 families were evicted in Ireland and that number had risen
considerably to 6,026 in 1847, while 9,657 families were removed in 1848.[78]
Clanricarde bluntly highlighted the landlord's position in a letter to
Clarendon in 1848. 'The landlords are prevented from aiding or tolerating
poor tenants. They are compelled to hunt out all such, to save their property
from the £4 clause.'[79]

The assassination of some Irish landowners, notably Denis Mahon,
consolidated English public opinion against the Irish peasantry and clergy, so
that 'the moralistic criticisms of Irish landowners took second place to the
demand that six million of Irish be disciplined'.[80] This shift in attitude by the
English public made clearances more acceptable to a British media that now
displayed sympathy for evicting Irish landlords rather than for those
dispossessed. By 1849, the *Illustrated London News*, which in the previous year
had described evictions as 'cruel and unjust in the extreme', now sent a
different message to its readers. 'We have no right, how great soever the
apparent or real hardship may be, to find fault with the landlord.' The paper
went on to defend the landlords.

> Truth is that these evictions ... are not merely a legal but natural process;
> and however much we may deplore the misery from which they spring,
> ... we cannot compel the Irish proprietor to continue in their miserable
> holdings the wretched swarms of people who pay no rent, and who
> prevent the improvement of property as long as they remain upon it.[81]

This change in public opinion allowed Irish landowners in cabinet to
adopt a hard-line attitude towards the necessity for large-scale evictions. In
1848, when Russell attempted to insert a clause into an Evicted Destitute bill
to regulate ejectments and to compensate evicted tenants for loss of tenure he
received a hostile response from the Irish ministers. Lord Palmerston forcefully
spelt out his view on the matter.

> It is useless to disguise the truth that any great improvement in the
> social system of Ireland must be founded upon an extensive change in

the present state of agrarian occupation, and that this change necessarily implies a long continued and systematic ejectment of small holders and squatting cottiers.[82]

Clanricarde's statement, outlining the current practice, brought 'a general shudder' from his colleagues in cabinet when the matter was discussed.

> There was no cure for the evil, if the tenant is not ejected by a certain day he claims the right to stay another year, and if he cannot be persuaded to go by that day light, nothing is left but to force him out by night and so he is forced out on a winter night and dies of cold and starvation by the roadside.[83]

Clanricarde told the house of lords that 'it was never his opinion that landlords should not evict bad tenants … but if the landlord wanted to get a good tenant off his land … he should not be permitted to do so without making him full compensation'.[84] This was inconsistent with his earlier objection to Stanley's Compensation bill.

In May 1848, Clanricarde took responsibility for moving the Evicted Destitute bill in the house of lords and he displayed little enthusiasm for the inclusion of any measure offensive to the landlord interest. In dealing with the provision which sought to oblige an evicting landlord to give prior notice to the poor law guardians, Clanricarde stated that if the range and scope of the measure were too extensive he would have no objection to limiting its operations.[85] His lack of conviction in handling the bill allowed his fellow Irish landowners to have several amendments inserted removing any of its proposals, restrictive to landlords. His lacklustre performance caused Clarendon to suspect that Clanricarde was protecting his fellow Galway gentry, a sentiment he expressed to Lord Lansdowne.[86]

While the overall objective of evictions and assisted emigration was to restructure Irish agriculture by the removal of defaulting tenants, it also had the effect of removing some enterprising farmers. The flight of strong tenant farmers from Ireland under the burden of high rents, heavy poor rates and low agricultural prices became a cause of alarm. In 1848, Clanricarde's agent informed Lloyd, a poor law inspector, that the greatest possible exertions were being made by the able-bodied labourers and mechanics to emigrate, and very many would accompany those going if they could they procure the means.[87] In December of that year Clanricarde expressed his concern that

> the U.S. will have gained enormous wealth and resources by the Irish famine and the poor law. All who should have tilled or should be tilling Irish soil in Mayo and Galway, which is left untilled, have been carried off to clear land in America.[88]

Clanricarde did not condemn or even criticise his fellow Galway landowners who were evicting tenants. He knew many of them personally through family connections and depended on their support at election time. He also believed that such clearances were necessary for the economic survival of estates. He contended that if emigration was properly funded by the state it would prove an effective and humane method of providing hope for the destitute masses while at the same time improving Irish agriculture thus saving many Irish landlords from insolvency. In 1850, in travelling through the Loughrea countryside, Osborne remarked, that 'there are not quite so many roofless gables by the roadside but quite enough marks of eviction left to show that the spirit still exists'.[89]

The Famine had several major long-term effects on Irish society, but none more striking than the demographic change that occurred in the decades during and immediately after the event. An examination of the demographic changes on Clanricarde's estate during the three decades 1841–71 demonstrates that major displacement of large sections of his tenantry took place. Griffith's Valuation of 1856 indicates the 166 townlands associated with Clanricarde's estate and the population can be determined from the 1851 census of Ireland and the 1871 census of Ireland abstracts.[90] While Clanricarde did not own all of these townlands, and Griffith's Valuation does not convey the exact area of land held by Clanricarde in the 1840s, nonetheless, the information extracted from these two primary sources allows reasonably accurate demographic comparisons to be made between his estate, Co. Galway and the country as a whole. An examination of the census records for the three decades 1841–51, 1851–61, and 1861–71 clearly demonstrates that the population decreases in each of these periods were more dramatic on Clanricarde's estate than those recorded for either of the other two geographical entities (Table 2).

Table 2. Population decrease of Ireland, Co. Galway and Clanricarde estate, 1841–71

| | Population Changes | | | |
	1841	1851	1861	1871
Ireland	8,175,238	6,515,794	5,798,967	5,412,377
Co. Galway	440, 98	321,684	271,478	248,458
Clanricarde Estate	21,929	13,924	10,937	9,699

Source: *Census of Ireland Abstracts, 1871*

During the 1841–51 decade, a 36 per cent decrease in population occurred on the estate, while the fertile parish of Lickmolassy, containing the town of

Portumna and Clanricarde's demesne, experienced a decline of 43 per cent in its population during the same period. The large rural parish of Ballinakill on the Woodford portion of his estate, with its poor quality land valued at an average of less than £0.2 per acre, saw its numbers decrease by 29 per cent in the 1841–51 period, a relatively small drop when compared with that for the Lickmolassy parish, the land of which had an average valuation of £0.67 per acre. Furthermore, the population decrease in the Lickmolassy parish was not uniform and certain townlands, such as Claggernagh East and Drumscar experienced massive depopulation during the Famine decade.[91] The population change in a sample of ten townlands from the parish illustrates this point (Table 3). It is questionable if such decreases could have been caused solely by the failure of the potato crop, famine deaths, voluntary emigration, or by paupers entering the workhouse at Loughrea. It is more likely that Clanricarde's agent singled out certain townlands of higher valuation for clearances to facilitate consolidation of holdings on the estate.

Clanricarde, unlike his cabinet colleagues, refrained from resorting to large-scale clearances to restructure his estate. Neither did he operate in a fashion similar to fellow east Galway landowner, Lord Dunsandle, who was nicknamed 'Lord Leveller',[92] because of the number of cabins he pulled down. However, notwithstanding the fact that the Loughrea union was not included in the twenty distressed unions needing extra assistance in the latter years of the Famine, the decrease in population was greater on Clanicarde's estate than in some of these destitute unions. Assisted emigration and small-scale ejectments, carried out by his agent, combined with the harsh effects of the Famine, gradually contributed to a substantial population decline. The population drop of 67 per cent in the Lickmolassy parish between 1841 and 1871 is consistent with Clanricarde's long-term objective of reducing numbers to facilitate land restructuring by consolidation.

Table 3. Population change in ten townlands in the Lickmolassy parish, 1841–51

Townland	Extent	1841	1851	% drop in population
	Acres			
Stoneyisland	557	254	126	50
Oldthort	471	248	164	32
Coolpowra	362	183	122	33
Drumscar	354	252	80	68
Gragueagown	294	159	97	39
Gurteenpeaddar	265	144	69	52
Graigueakilleen	244	122	64	48
Claggernagh East	238	247	31	87
Ballyshrule	224	87	50	43
Shanvally	211	166	100	40

Source: *Census of Ireland, 1851*

4. Conclusion

During the years 1846–52, Clanricarde reached the pinnacle of his political career as a minister in Lord John Russell's administration. From an early stage in his political life, he displayed a good working knowledge of, and interest in, Irish affairs. His loyal service to the Liberal party led to his appointment as ambassador to Russia in 1838 and he was held in sufficiently high esteem to be appointed to Russell's cabinet ahead of many of his colleagues as one of three landlords with major Irish estates. This gave Clanricarde the opportunity to represent his landed class and help shape Irish policy from within the government. He contributed fully to many House of Lords debates and took principled positions on the great policy issues of the day. In his personal life, Clanricarde was not a loyal husband and many considered him a man of reckless and spendthrift habits. Although popular with his peers in parliament, these aspects of his character were unacceptable to them and eventually led to his political demise. To assess Clanricarde's performance as cabinet minister, and major landowner, his political philosophy and handling of a number of issues of local and national importance must be evaluated.

Most of Clanricarde's actions can be attributed to his rational and rather benign pursuit of his objective of maintaining the political supremacy and dominant position of his aristocratic class through the controlling influence of the Irish landed gentry over its tenants. He was keen to pass on to his heirs a 52,000-acre estate which had been bequeathed to him by his father and to continue the proud family tradition in Co. Galway. In electoral politics, Clanricarde supported the party that would best protect his interests and he arranged, by all conventional means, to have sympathetic representatives, both locally and at Westminster.

In the religious domain, Clanricarde did not permit ancient animosities to compromise the pursuit of his goal. Although raised in the protestant faith, he was a committed emancipationist and did not support the proselytising activities of successive earls of Clancarty on the nearby Garbally estate in Ballinasloe. He was benevolent to Catholic causes locally and contributed liberally towards the construction of Catholic churches for the tenants on his estate. He campaigned for the endowment of Maynooth College and the payment of the Catholic clergy. Clanricarde was also committed to the establishment of an educated Irish peasantry. He was a strong advocate of the national school system which he supported by providing school sites and financial resources towards teachers salaries. His reputation for tolerance and the occasional well-reported local donation promoted tenant loyalty and discouraged fundamentalist enthusiasms that could threaten the religious equilibrium in Co. Galway. Like Russell, he realised that equal rights and privileges must be granted to a largely Catholic Irish population in order to guarantee its loyalty to the crown.

Clanricarde was one of the most outspoken critics in parliament of a poor law system for Ireland in the years following its introduction in 1838. He realised, but failed to convince his cabinet colleagues, that such a system would not work in Ireland. His opposition to that law, enacted by his own party, was based on his strongly held belief that such a system was not appropriate for Ireland due to the poverty of the country, its social structure and the huge expense involved in delivering relief by that means. He favoured the introduction of many of the recommendations of the earlier poor inquiry which he argued would have been far more effective in addressing Ireland's problems of overpopulation, underdevelopment and a subsistence economy. Once in government, however, Clanricarde accepted the poor law system as a vehicle to relieve destitution in Ireland. After initial objections by himself and his moderate Liberal colleagues, he reluctantly endorsed the 1847 Poor Law Amendment Act which made Irish property pay for Irish poverty. He realised that he had no chance of resisting its implementation against the more powerful 'moralist' wing of the cabinet, despite the 'moderates' objection to any further burden of rates on property. Indeed, he even called for legislation to compel Irish landowners to pay their fair share towards the support of the poor.

Clanricarde continually highlighted the desperate plight of the Irish starving masses in his correspondence with Russell, Clarendon and others associated with the Irish administration. He lobbied strongly for state assistance to relieve distress through a range of measures such as public works and land drainage. He sought to have corn depots set up in each of his towns of Loughrea and Portumna in order to have control over the distribution of food locally. He donated generously to many local relief committees and invested considerable money in the assisted emigration of his tenants in the years before the Famine. He strongly urged the prime minister to provide for state assisted emigration but Clanricarde and its other proponents were unable to break down Trevelyan's opposition to such intervention. While this policy would not have removed the necessity for other kinds of public relief during the Famine, Clanricarde believed that, if properly and humanely managed, it would prove a viable form of relief and save countless lives in the west of Ireland. Such a scheme would also have been beneficial to himself by removing poorer tenants from his estate and allowing for the restructuring and consolidation of its holdings. However, Clanricarde did not authorize or initiate any private schemes of work locally to alleviate the destitution of his tenants. In that regard, he did not match the efforts of some of his neighbouring Galway landlords.

The 1847 Act provided for the appointment of relieving officers, but Clanricarde, although in agreement with the principle of the measure, vehemently resisted their appointment in his own union, notwithstanding the fact that paupers had died there from starvation. His objection to the appointment of these paid officials was designed to minimise the poor rate burden in his union even if this resulted in the loss of life. The refusal of the Loughrea board of guardians to appoint relieving officers led to its dissolution and the institution of a sworn inquiry. The evidence to that inquiry, provided by the newly appointed vice guardians and others associated with Loughrea workhouse clearly indicated the gross neglect of the union's affairs and the appalling state of its workhouse and inmates. Despite this, Clanricarde continued to object to the appointment of vice-guardians thereby further adding to the misery of the destitute peasantry.

Although he was lord lieutenant of the county, and therefore, its legal authority, Clanricarde stopped short of condemning the large-scale evictions by his fellow Galway landowners, Gerrard, St George and Blake. Clanricarde's enthusiastic support for the 'Gregory Clause' illustrated his desire to rid his estate of defaulting tenants and in cabinet he even defended the rights of landlords to carry out evictions. However, unlike Palmerston and Lansdowne, he did not carry out such massive clearances on his own estate. Instead he resorted to small-scale displacement over a long period of time and local newspapers reported that ejectments were taking place from his Galway property under the watchful eye of his agent. This contributed to the percentage decrease in population on his estate being higher than those for Co. Galway or the country.

As a major landowner, Clanricarde did little to progress the improvement of agriculture on his estate. His cavalier approach to the management of his estate left a legacy of discontent amongst his tenantry. He ignored the several complaints of his agent's misconduct in granting leases to the tenants. Clarendon reference to the neglect on Clanricarde's estate at Portumna did nothing to enhance his perceived reputation among his peers as an improving landowner. He did not carry out any major improvements on his estate and many of the goals he had set for land restructuring were not realised. His appalling neglect of Loughrea underlined his lack of interest in the improvement of that town and its inhabitants.

During the Famine period, Clanricarde was committed to reforming the relationship between landlord and tenant. He was prepared to concede certain legal rights to tenants, such as compensation for improvements, and he proposed a system of redress for tenants against oppressive landlords. He believed that cottiers should not be given leases but instead be given employment on estates. However, as a major landlord with an obvious bias towards his own class, he was adamant that 'fixity of tenure' should not be enshrined in any government legislation. His political philosophy was guided by the underlying principle that the rights and privileges of landed proprietors should be upheld at all times. He opposed any government measure that threatened to infringe upon the sanctity of property rights and contract law. He also strongly objected to Trevelyan's proposal to carve up estates into smaller lots, seeing this as an attempt to undermine the dominant position of major landowners.

These positions may help to explain why Clanricarde, the spokesman for policies to promote responsible landlordship and agricultural development, so neglected to improve his market towns, particularly Loughrea, and largely failed to improve the farming potential of his own estate. His apparent inconsistency in not investing in the town of Loughrea probably related to his desire to promote the emigration of marginal tenants from his lands. He may have concluded that to improve conditions at Loughrea would undermine this objective by providing a more palatable destination for tenants who would otherwise move far enough away to be unlikely to return. Similarly, he may also have worried that a high profile expansion in productive acreage on his land would provide false hope for those who would otherwise emigrate. Furthermore, he might well have calculated that, until government adopted policies that would provide a higher return to agricultural investment, it simply was not a financially wise use of available family resources.

Although Clanricarde may not have been a great philanthropic landlord, dedicated to redistributing his wealth among the needy on his estate, neither was he a malevolent incompetent. His position on the poor law, uniform taxation and government-assisted emigration were, from among the options discussed at the time of the Famine, the most economically beneficial for landowners in the west and south of Ireland. He constantly emphasised to government the need to promote efficiency in agriculture and capital markets. It is unlikely that the Famine substantially changed Clanricarde's views on appropriate government policies and his overriding objective likely remained intact. What he saw during the Famine probably reinforced his beliefs on property rights, contract law and the need for economic incentives. Therefore, Clanricarde's failings in relation to Ireland during the Famine were those of omission rather than commission.

Clanricarde's rational pursuit of his understandable objective of main-taining the dominant position of his class, largely within the law and social mores of the day, was not unique among the leading figures in Ireland and Britain in the decades prior to the Great Famine. If it can be demonstrated in local histories that such behaviour was the norm, it would support the proposition that one of western Europe's most tragic episodes was allowed to happen less by misguided policies than by the inevitable playing out of demographic, agricultural and economic forces in the context of the social and land ownership regime in Ireland in the first half of the nineteenth century.

Notes

ABBREVIATIONS

Harewood/ Clanricarde	Clanricarde Papers in the Harewood Collection, Leeds
JGAHS	*Journal of the Galway Archaeological and Historical Society*
NA	National Archives, Dublin
NLI	National Library of Ireland
NUIG	National University of Ireland, Galway
PRO	Public Record Office
RLFC	Relief Commission
WYAS	West Yorkshire Archives Service

INTRODUCTION

1 J.S. Donnelly, *The great Irish potato Famine* (Stroud, 2001), p.115.

2 P. Gray, *Famine, land and politics: British government and Irish society, 1843–50* (Dublin, 1999), passim.

3 D.A. Kerr, *'A nation of beggars'?: priests, people, and politics in famine Ireland, 1846–1852* (Oxford, 1994), pp 25, 275.

4 C. Kinealy, *This great calamity: the Irish Famine, 1845–52* (Dublin, 1994), p. 216.

1. THE FIRST MARQUIS OF CLANRICARDE (1802–74)

1 D. Kearns, 'Who are the Clanricardes?' in M. Shiel and D. Roche (ed.), *Clanricarde country and the land campaign* (Woodford, 1987), p.11.

2 B. Cunnigham, 'From warlords to landlords: political and social change in Galway, 1540–1640' in G. Moran (ed.), *Galway history and society: interdisciplinary essays on the history of an Irish county* (Dublin, 1996), pp 97–129. See also B. Cunningham, 'Richard Burke (c.1572– 1635) and the lordship of Clanricard' in J. Fenlon (ed.), *Portumna castle* (Dublin, forthcoming).

3 John Lowe (ed.), *Letter-book of the earl of Clanricarde, 1643–47* (Dublin, 1983), p. v.

4 Michael MacMahon, *Portumna castle and its lords* (Portumna, 2000), pp 25–6.

5 The atrocities committed by the 'Black and Tans' in Ireland during the war of independence caused the Connaught Rangers to mutiny in India in 1920, and the regiment was finally disbanded in 1922. See MacMahon, *Portumna castle*, p. 28.

6 T. Dooley, *The decline of the big house in Ireland* (Dublin, 2001), p. 30.

7 To avoid confusion the appellation 'Clanricarde' will hereafter be applied to Ulick John de Burgh.

8 G.E. Cockayne, *The complete peerage of England, Scotland, Ireland, Great Britain and the United Kingdom: extant, extinct or dormant* (13 vols., London, 1913), iii, p. 238.

9 J. Foster, *Alumni Oxonienses: the members of the university of Oxford, 1715–1886: their parentage, birthplace, and year of birth, with a record of their degrees* (London, 1888), i, p. 193.

10 Cockayne, *Complete peerage* iii, p. 238.

11 Gregory was a major south Galway landowner and MP for the county and was responsible for the introduction of the 'quarter acre clause' in 1847 which was commonly named after him. See B. Jenkins, *Sir William Gregory of Coole: biography of an Anglo-Irishman* (Buckinghamshire, 1986), p. 82.

12 D. Englefield, J. Seaton and I. White, *Facts about the British prime ministers* (New York, 1995), p. 110.

13 WYAS, Leeds, Harewood/Clanricarde papers, bundle 8, Lord Dudley to Clanricarde, 13 Aug. 1827.

14 Cockayne, *Complete peerage* iii, p. 238.
15 Englefield et al., *Facts about the British prime ministers*, p. 143.
16 Roche, 'The later Clanricardes', in Shiel and Roche (eds), *Clanricarde country*, pp 17–28.
17 Cockayne, *Complete peerage* iii, p. 238.
18 WYAS, Leeds, Harewood/Clanricarde papers, bundle 50, anonymous letter to Canning (undated). See also T. Feeney, 'The Woodford evictions' (unpublished MEd thesis, NUIG, 1976), p. 4.
19 T. P. O'Connor, *Memoirs of an old parliamentarian* (2 vols., London, 1929), ii, p. 122. Henry Labouchere MP was chief secretary of Ireland (1846–7).
20 He developed a reputation for socializing in the company of his henchman Tom Nolan known as 'Tom the devil'. See Knight of Glin, D. J. Griffin and N.K. Robinson, *Vanishing houses of Ireland* (Dublin, 1988), p. 17.
21 A number of the contributors to 200 hours of video footage firmly believed and recalled accounts passed on to them by their elders of the unfavourable treatment meted out to the daughters of Clanricarde's tenants while they were employed at his residence in Portumna. In 1990, the novelist Joy Martin, in her book, *Ulick's daughter,* fictionalized his alleged association with the daughter of one of his tenants.
22 *United Ireland*, 16 Oct. 1886.
23 *An inquiry into the truth of the accusations made against the marquis of Clanricarde: Handcock v. Delacour, lately heard in the Irish court of chancery* (Dublin, 1855). See also J. Greaney, *Dunmore* (Dunmore, 1984), pp 51–67.
24 Roche, 'The later Clanricardes', in Shiel and Roche, *Clanricarde country*, p. 25.
25 *The Times*, 23 Feb. 1858.
26 See, for example, WYAS, Leeds, Harewood/Clanricarde papers, bundles 33, 50 and 76.
27 WYAS, Leeds, Harewood/Clanricarde papers, bundle 3, A. H. Blake to Clanricarde, 26 May 1836.
28 B. Walker, *Election results in Ireland, 1801–1922* (Dublin, 1978), p. 283.
29 *Royal commission of inquiry into the state of law and practice in respect of the occupation of land in Ireland: report, minutes of evidence, part II*, HC 1845 [616], xx, p.561 (Hereafter cited as the *Devon Commission, minutes of evidence*).
30 Richard Griffith, *General valuation of rateable property in Ireland* (Dublin, 1856).

31 *The parliamentary gazetteer of Ireland* (3 vols., Dublin, 1846), ii, p. 695.
32 C. Kinealy, 'The response of the poor law to the great Famine in Co. Galway' in Moran (ed.), *Galway history and society*, p. 390.
33 *Parliamentary Gazetteer*, ii, p. 695.
34 Kinealy, 'The response of the poor law to the great Famine in Co. Galway', p. 390.
35 J. O'Connor, *The workhouses of Ireland* (Dublin, 1995), p. 66.
36 *Tuam Herald*, 19 May 1838.
37 *Hansard*, xlii, col. 722, 1 May 1838. See also *Hansard,* xliii, col. 360, 28 May 1838.
38 *Hansard*, xliii, col. 360, 28 May 1838.
39 *Hansard*, xliii, cols. 475–6, 28 May 1838.
40 *Hansard*, xliv, col. 12, 9 July 1838.
41 *Hansard*, lxvi, cols. 191–2, 6 Feb 1843.
42 *Hansard*, lxviii, col. 1349, 8 May 1843.
43 Ibid., cols. 1349–50,
44 *First report from his majesty's commissioners for enquiring into the condition of the poorer in Ireland, with appendix (A) and supplement.* HC 1835 (369), xxxii part I, p.1.
45 *Hansard*, lxviii, col. 1352, 8 May 1843.
46 Ibid., col. 1386.
47 *Hansard*, lxxiv, col. 204, 23 April 1844.
48 Ibid., cols. 894–5.
49 C. Kinealy, *This great calamity*, p. 101.
50 *Hansard*, lxxvi, cols. 7–11, 27 June 1844.
51 *Hansard*, lxxxii, col.135, 8 July 1845.
52 See Kinealy, 'The response of the poor law to the great Famine in Co. Galway', p. 376.
53 NA, RLFC2/Z13210, Inspector Lewis to inspector general, Dublin Castle, 22 Sept. 1845.
54 NA, RLFC2/Z15250, Police report, Marble Hill, Loughrea, 6 Nov. 1845.
55 NA, RLFC2/Z17066, Clanricarde to Sir Thomas Freemantle, 30 Nov. 1845.
56 C. Kinealy, 'The response of the poor law', p. 45
57 See C. Ó'Gráda, *Black '47 and beyond: the great Irish Famine in history, economy, and memory* (New Jersey, 1999), pp 49–53.
58 NA, RLFC2/Z17066, Clanricarde to Sir Thomas Freemantle, 30 Nov. 1845.
59 Ibid.
60 NA, RLFC3/1/1274, Clanricarde to John Pitt Kennedy, 7 Apr. 1846.
61 NA, RLFC3/1/852, Clanricarde to John Pitt Kennedy, 21 Mar. 1846.
62 Ibid.
63 NA, RLFC3/2/11/89, Clanricarde to Lord Heytesbury, 3 April 1846.
64 NA, RLFC2/Z5268, Ambrose O'Kelly to Lord Lincoln, 7 March 1846.
65 Letter from Mary Kelly to her children and grandchildren, Gurtray 1943, quoted

in J.J. Conwell, *Lickmolassy by the Shannon* (Portumna, 1998), pp 72–5.

66 NA, RLFC3/2/11/9, Ambrose O'Kelly to relief commission, 16 April 1846.

67 NA, RLFC3/1/1274, Clanricarde to John Pitt Kennedy, 7 April 1846.

68 Denis Hynes to Randolph Routh, 12 Jan 1847, quoted in Conwell, *Lickmolassy by the Shannon*, p. 86.

69 NA, RLFC3/1/1089, P. Hobart to inspector general, 28 March 1846.

70 NA, RLFC3/1/3857, Capt. S. R. Pole to Randolph Routh, 29 June 1846.

71 Ibid.

72 NA, RLFC3/1/491, Clanricarde to John Pitt Kennedy, 5 Feb 1846.

73 Ibid.

74 *Hansard*, lxxxiii, col. 745, 12 Feb 1846.

75 *Hansard*, lxxxiv, cols. 1006, 1189, 13, 18 March 1846; *Hansard*, lxxxv, cols. 293, 403, 485, 703–710, 98 1, 30 March 1846; 1, 2, 17, 24 April 1846.

76 This may have been Clanricarde's cousin, Sir Thomas Burke from Marble Hill.

77 WYAS, Leeds, Harewood/Clanricarde papers, bundle 71, anonymous letter to Capt. Burke, 3 March 1846.

78 PRO, Russell papers, 30/22/5A, fols. 164–6, Clanricarde to Lord John Russell, 11 March 1846.

2. CABINET MINISTER DURING THE FAMINE

1 PRO, Russell papers, 30/22/4E, fols. 253–4, Clanricarde to Lord John Russell, 21 Dec. 1845.

2 Ibid.

3 Ibid.

4 Kerr, '*A nation of beggars*'?, p. 6.

5 Gray, *Famine, land and politics*, p. 63.

6 P. Gray, 'Ideology and the Famine' in Cathal Póirtéir (ed.), *The great Irish Famine* (Dublin, 1995), p. 89.

7 Gray, *Famine, land and politics*, pp 22–5. Lansdowne's Irish estate was located in Co. Kerry while Monteagle owned extensive property in Co. Limerick. Palmerston had his Irish estate in Co. Sligo.

8 Gray, 'Ideology and the Famine', p. 90.

9 NA, RLFC2/Z17066, Clanricarde to Sir Thomas Freemantle, 30 Nov. 1845.

10 Gray, 'Ideology and the Famine', p. 92.

11 For more on the divisions within Russell's cabinet see Gray, *Famine, land and politics*, p. 26.

12 *Tuam Herald*, 17 Apr. 1841. Redington had undertaken the management of the races

of Loughrea. Clanricarde and his uncle, Sir John Burke, circulated insinuations that Redington organized the races to render himself popular with a view to representing Co. Galway.

13 J. Murphy, *The Redingtons of Clarinbridge* (Clarinbridge, 1999), p. 67.

14 Gray, 'Ideology and the Famine', p. 91.

15 P.K. Egan, *The parish of Ballinasloe* (Dublin, 1960), pp 175–223. See also evidence of the Revd John Macklin in *Devon commission, minutes of evidence, part II*, HC [616], xx, p. 561.

16 *Hansard*, lxxxiv, cols.1408–9, 23 March 1846.

17 *Hansard*, xli, cols. 318–19, 1 March 1848.

18 *Hansard*, lxiii, col. 970, 30 May 1842.

19 *Tuam Herald*, 24 Feb 1844.

20 Ibid.

21 Ibid.

22 *Hansard*, lxxi, col. 6, 31 July 1843.

23 *Hansard*, lxx, cols. 1099–1138, 14 July 1843. Lord French had attended and chaired a Repeal meeting at Caltra on 21 May 1843 which adopted a motion for the repeal of the Act of Union. See Marty Gilmore and Mattie Kilroy, *The history of Ahascragh and Caltra* (Caltra, 1996), p. 85.

24 WYAS, Leeds, Harewood/Clanricarde papers, bundle 79. Clanricarde to Clarendon, Aug 1847; see also *Hansard*, xcvi, col. 892, 18 Feb 1848.

25 WYAS, Leeds, Harewood/Clanricarde papers, bundle 79. Clanricarde to Clarendon, Aug 1847.

26 PRO, Russell papers, 30/22/7B, fols.192–5, Clanricarde to Russell, April 1848.

27 Ibid.

28 *Hansard*, ci, col.123, 14 Aug 1848.

29 *Hansard*, cxx, cols. 873–9, 18 April 1852.

30 *Hansard*, cxix, col. 1132, 17 Feb 1852.

31 *Hansard*, cxviii, cols. 1264–5, 22 July 1851.

32 John Prest, *Lord John Russell* (London, 1972), pp 429–30.

33 Bodleian library, Oxford, Clarendon papers, deposit Irish box 9, Clanricarde to Clarendon, 23 March 1851.

34 NA, EDI/35, Gortanumera National school, 8 Feb 1860; the inspector dealing with the application to build a new National school at Gortanumera in 1860 noted that the landowner, the marquis of Clanricarde, was 'a good friend to education', not only had he granted six school sites on his estate and subscribed to the erection of the schoolhouses, but had also contributed liberally towards the payment of the teacher salaries.

35 *Tuam Herald*, 7 Jan 1843. For further examples of Clanricarde's benevolence see

also *Slater's national commercial directory of Ireland* (Dublin, 1856), p. 153; S. Lewis, *A topographical dictionary of Ireland* (2 vols., London, 1837), ii, pp 317, 469.

36 The countess was 90 years of age when she died in 1854.

37 Conwell, *Lickmolassy by the Shannon*, p. 50.

38 PRO, Russell papers, 30/22/6B, fol. 254–7, Clanricarde to Bessborough, 16 Mar. 1847.

39 Ibid.

40 Ibid.

41 Ibid.

42 Ibid.

43 Quoted in Jenkins, *Sir William Gregory*, p. 76.

44 Bessborough to Clanricarde, 19 March 1847, quoted in Jenkins, *Sir William Gregory*, p. 76.

45 PRO, Russell papers, 30/22/6B, fols. 254–7 and 268, Bessborough to Russell, 19 March 1847.

46 Jenkins, *Sir William Gregory*, p. 80.

47 Ibid., p. 118.

48 WYAS, Leeds, Harewood/Clanricarde papers, bundle 76, Clanricarde to Denis Daly, 8 July 1847. J. J. Bodkin had been Liberal MP for Co. Galway from 1835 and Christopher St George was elected Tory MP in the 1847 election.

49 James Henry Monahan had served as Irish solicitor general (1846–7). See Gray, *Famine, land and politics*, p. 374.

50 PRO, Russell papers, 30/22/6B, fols. 37–8, Clanricarde to Russell, April 1847.

51 Walker, *Election results in Ireland, 1801–1922*, p. 283. See also Gray, *Famine, land and politics*, p. 374.

52 Jenkins, *Sir William Gregory*, p. 119.

53 *The Nation*, 13 June 1847.

54 Ibid.

55 PRO, Russell papers, 30/22/4E, fol. 280, Clanricarde to Russell, 23 Dec 1845.

56 Ibid. See also 30/22/5A, fols. 207–10, Clanricarde to Russell, 17 Dec 1846.

57 PRO, Russell papers, 30/22/5A, fols. 207–10, Clanricarde to Russell, 17 Dec 1846.

58 Ibid.

59 PRO, Russell papers, 30/22/6A, fol. 95, Clanricarde to Russell, 8 Jan 1847.

60 Ibid.

61 Gray, *Famine, land and politics*, pp 229–30.

62 PRO, London, Russell papers, 30/22/6A, fol. 94, Clanricarde to Russell, 8 Jan 1847.

63 Ibid., 30/22/7B, fol. 194, Clanricarde to Russell, April 1847.

64 WYAS, Leeds, Harewood/Clanricarde papers, bundle 79, Clanricarde to Clarendon, 16 Aug 1847.

65 Ibid.

66 Gray, *Famine, land and politics*, p. 236.

67 Ibid., pp 231–4.

68 *Hansard*, xci, cols. 479–80, 22 Mar. 1847.

69 *Hansard*, xcii, cols.1046, 18 May 1847.

70 *Hansard*, xcii, cols.106–7, 29 Apr. 1847.

71 O'Connor, *The workhouses of Ireland*, p. 263.

72 *Hansard*, xcii, col. 505, 7 May 1847.

73 *Papers relating to proceedings for the relief of distress and the state of unions and workhouses in Ireland* (sixth series), HC 1847–8 [955], lv, Robert Darcy to Owen Lloyd, 28 April 1848, pp 901–2.

74 WYAS, Leeds, Harewood/Clanricarde papers, bundle 48, Clarendon to Clanricarde, 7 June 1848.

75 Bodleian Library, Oxford, Clarendon papers, deposit Irish box 9, Clanricarde to Clarendon, 5 June 1848.

76 WYAS, Leeds, Harewood/Clanricarde papers, bundle 79, Clanricarde to Clarendon, 16 Aug. 1847.

77 *Hansard*, cv, col. 286, 11 May 1849.

78 Ibid.

79 Ibid.

80 *Hansard*, ciii, cols. 1178–9, 23 March 1849.

81 Ibid., cols. 1186.

82 PRO, London, Russell papers, 30/22/8C, fols. 171–2, Clanricarde to Russell, 3 Jan 1850.

83 Ibid.

84 *Hansard*, lxxii, cols. 34–5, 1 Feb 1844.

85 *Hansard*, lxxiii, cols. 571–3, 5 March 1844.

86 *Hansard*, lxxxi, col. 229, 9 June 1845.

87 PRO, London, Russell papers, 30/22/6H, fol. 226, Clanricarde to Russell, Mar. 1847.

88 WYAS, Leeds, Harewood/Clanricarde papers, bundle 79, Clarendon to Clanricarde, 13 Aug. 1847.

89 Gray, *Famine, land and politics*, p.171.

90 WYAS, Leeds, Harewood/Clanricarde papers, bundle 79, Clanricarde to Clarendon, 16 Aug 1847.

91 Bodleian Library, Oxford, Clarendon papers, deposit Irish box 9, Clanricarde to Clarendon, 6 Sept. 1847.

92 Ibid.

93 WYAS, Leeds, Harewood/Clanricarde papers, bundle 76, Clanricarde to Somerville, 17 Sept 1847.

94 Bodleian Library, Oxford, Clarendon papers, deposit Irish box 9, Clanricarde to Clarendon, 6 Sept 1847.

95 Ibid.

96 Ibid.

97 PRO, Russell papers, 30/22/2B, fol. 207, Clanricarde to Russell, 17 Dec 1846. See also PRO, Russell papers, 30/22/7B, fol. 193, Apr. 1847.

98 Jonathan Pim (1806–85), a Dublin draper and textile manufacturer, was joint secretary of the central relief committee of the Society of Friends during the Famine. He later became the first Quaker to sit in parliament as a Liberal MP for Dublin (1865–74).

99 PRO, Russell papers, 30/22/7B, fol. 194, Clanricarde to Russell, April 1847.

100 *Hansard*, cxxviii, col.787–8, 27 June 1853.

3. CLANRICARDE'S ESTATE AND THE FAMINE

1 *Devon commission, minutes of evidence, part II*, HC 1845 [616], xx, p. 559.

2 Jordan, *Killtullagh/Killimordaly*, p. 35.

3 *Devon commission, minutes of evidence, part II*, HC 1845 [616], xx, pp 559–65.

4 Jordan, *Killtullagh/Killimordaly*, p.39.

5 *Tuam Herald*, 9 Feb 1839.

6 *Devon commission, minutes of evidence, part II*, HC 1845 [616], xx, pp 556–73.

7 Ibid.

8 *Galway Advertiser*, 16 Feb 1839.

9 *Devon commission, minutes of evidence, part II*, HC 1845 [616], xx, p.566.

10 *Galway Advertiser*, 16 Feb1839. See also *Tuam Herald*, 16 Feb 1839.

11 *Devon commission, minutes of evidence, part II*, HC 1845 [616], xx, p. 559.

12 Ibid.

13 NLI, F. S. Bourke collection, Ms. 10,736, *Gleanings in the west of Ireland: a blotter of an account in seven long letters of a journey by canal from Dublin to Shannon harbour and thence to Galway* (1838).

14 *Tuam Herald*, 9 Feb 1839.

15 *Devon commission, minutes of evidence, part II*, HC 1845 [616], xx, pp 563, 564, 565, 571.

16 *The parliamentary gazetteer of Ireland* (3 vols., Dublin, London and Edinburgh, 1846), ii, pp 696–7.

17 *Papers relating to proceedings for the relief of distress and the state of unions and workhouses in Ireland (Sixth series)*, HC 1847–8 [955], lv, vice-guardians to poor law commissioners, 7 Aug 1848, p. 110.

18 Ibid.

19 Bodleian library, Oxford, Clarendon papers, deposit Irish box, letterbook v, Clarendon to Russell, 19 Dec 1849.

20 PRO, Russell papers, 30/22/6/A, fol. 95, Clanricarde to Russell, 8 Jan 1847. See also *Hansard*, xcii, col. 441, 6 May 1847; *Hansard*, civ, col. 1257, 4 May 1849.

21 *Hansard*, xcii, col. 491, 7 May 1847.

22 WYAS, Leeds, Harewood/Clanricarde papers, bundle 74, Clanricarde to Redington, 7 Aug 1847.

23 Ibid. bundle 79, Clanricarde to Clarendon, 16 Aug 1847.

24 Ibid., bundle 76, Clanricarde to Somerville, 18 Sept 1847.

25 Ibid., bundle 75, Somerville to Clanricarde, 27 Sept 1847.

26 Michael McMahon, 'The Famine in Loughrea poor law union' in Shiel and Roche (eds.), *A forgotten campaign*, pp 161–7.

27 PRO, Russell papers, 30/22/7B, Clanricarde to Russell, March 1848.

28 *Papers relating to proceedings for the relief of distress and the state of unions and workhouses in Ireland (Sixth series)*, HC 1847–8 [955], lv, vice-guardians to the poor law commissioners, 28 Feb 1848, p. 874.

29 Ibid.

30 *Papers relating to proceedings for the relief of distress and the state of unions and workhouses in Ireland (Sixth series)*, HC 1847–8 [955], lv, vice-guardians to the poor law commissioners, 28 Feb. 1848, p. 873.

31 *Papers relating to proceedings for the relief of distress and the state of unions and workhouses in Ireland (Sixth series)*, HC 1847–8 [955], lv, vice-guardians to the poor law commissioners, 28 Feb. 1848, p. 891.

32 Ibid., Mr. Lloyd to the poor law commissioners, 20 May 1848, p. 893.

33 *Papers relating to proceedings for the relief of distress and the state of unions and workhouses in Ireland (Sixth series)*, HC 1847–8 [955], lv, Rev Thomas Burke to Mr Lloyd, 3 May 1848, p. 903

34 WYAS, Leeds, Harewood/Clanricarde papers, bundle 79, Clanricarde to Clarendon, 16 Aug 1847.

35 *Papers relating to proceedings for the relief of distress and the state of unions and workhouses in Ireland (Sixth series)*, HC 1847–8 [955], lv, Bishop John Derry to Mr Lloyd, 28 April 1848, pp 906–8.

36 Ibid.

37 Ibid.

38 PRO, Russell papers, 30/22/8C, Clanricarde to Russell, fols. 329–330, 10 Feb 1850.

39 James Donnelly Jnr., 'Mass evictions and the great Famine' in Cathal Póirtéir (ed.), *The great Irish Famine*, p. 156. See Cormac O'Grada, *Black '47 and beyond: the great Irish Famine in history, economy, and memory* (New Jersey, 1999), pp 104–121.

40 W. E.Vaughan and A. J. Fitzpatrick (eds.), *Irish historical statistics* (Dublin, 1978), p. 260.

41 Kinealy, *This great calamity: the Irish Famine 1845–52*, pp 309–30.

42 Marquis of Sligo to Lord Monteagle, 8 Oct 1848, quoted in Woodham-Smith, *The great hunger*, p. 364.

43 *Tuam Herald*, 26 Oct 1839.

44 *Devon commission, minutes of evidence, part II*, HC 1845 [616], xx, p. 561.

45 Ibid., xx, p. 560.

46 Ibid., p. 558.

47 Ibid., pp 556–77.

48 Ibid., pp 565–69.

49 WYAS, Leeds, Harewood/Clanricarde papers, bundle 79,. Thomas Doolan to Daily Star, 25 May 1847.

50 PRO, Russell papers, 30/22/5F, fol. 207 Clanricarde to Russell, 17 Dec 1846.

51 PRO, Russell papers, 30/22/6A, fols. 94–5, Clanricarde to Russell, 8 Jan 1847.

52 *Hansard*, lxxxv, cols. 273–4, 30 March 1846.

53 Ibid., cols. 273–4.

54 Ibid., col. 287.

55 Walker, *Election results in Ireland, 1801–1922*, p. 283.

56 Joseph Murphy, *The Redingtons of Clarinbridge*, (Galway, 1999), p. 139–40.

57 *Illustrated London News*, 1 April 1848.

58 Ibid.

59 *Hansard*, xcix, col. 82, 30 March 1848.

60 *The Nation*, 15 April 1848.

61 *Papers relating to proceedings for the relief of distress and the state of unions and workhouses in Ireland (Sixth series)*, HC 1847–8 [955], lv, Bishop Derry to Owen Lloyd, 28 April 1848, p. 907.

62 Russell to Clarendon, 27 March 1848, quoted in Gray, *Famine, land and politics*, p.191.

63 Stephen J. Campbell, *The great Irish Famine* (Strokestown, 1994), pp 45–4.

64 Russell to Clarendon, 15 Nov 1847, quoted in Kerr, '*A nation of beggars*'?, p. 88.

65 Woodham-Smith, *The great hunger*, pp 227–30.

66 Gerard J. Lyne, *The Lansdowne estate in Kerry under W. S. Trench 1849–72* (Dublin, 2001). See also Kinealy, *This great calamity: the Irish Famine 1845–52*, pp 313–14.

67 *The Times*, 10 April 1847.

68 *The Times*, 10 March 1847.

69 *Illustrated London News*, 20 Feb 1847.

70 Ibid., 20 March 1847.

71 *Hansard*, lxxxix, col. 612, 1 Feb 1847.

72 *Hansard*, xci, col. 255, 22 March 1847.

73 *Illustrated London News*, 23 Jan 1847.

74 Donnelly, *The great Irish potato Famine*, pp 93–4.

75 *Hansard*, xci, col. 256, 22 March 1847.

76 *Hansard*, xcii, col.106, 29 April 1847.

77 WYAS, Leeds, Harewood/Clanricarde papers, bundle 76, Clanricarde to Somerville, 18 Aug 1847.

78 Kerr, '*A nation of beggars*'?, p.137.

79 Clanricarde to Clarendon, 31 Dec 1848, quoted in Woodham-Smith, *The great hunger*, p. 364.

80 Gray, *Famine, land and politics*, p. 182.

81 *Illustrated London News*, 20 Oct 1849.

82 Palmerston memo: 'State of Ireland', 31 March 1848, quoted in Gray, *Famine, land and politics*, p. 192.

83 Diary of Lord Broughton, 25 March 1848, quoted in Kerr, '*A nation of beggars*'?, p. 137.

84 *Hansard*, ci, col. 258, 18 Aug 1848.

85 *Hansard*, xcix, col. 82, 30 May 1848.

86 Clarendon to G. Grey, 17, 18 June 1848, quoted in Gray, *Famine, land and politics*, p. 193.

87 *Papers relating to proceedings for the relief of distress and the state of unions and workhouses in Ireland (Sixth series)*, HC 1847–8 [955], lv, Robert D'Arcy to Owen Lloyd, 28 April 1848, p. 903.

88 Clanricarde to Clarendon, 21 Dec 1848, quoted in Woodham-Smith, *The great hunger*, p. 367.

89 S. Godolphin Osborne, *Gleanings in the west of Ireland* (London, 1850), p. 43.

90 *Comparative view of census of Ireland, 1841–1851*. HC 1852, [373] xlvi, pp 368, 362. Also *Census of Ireland 1871: abstract of enumerator's returns* HC 1871 [375], lix, p. 801.

91 The townland of Drumcsar later became noted for its horseracing course.

92 Jordan, *Killtullagh/Killimordaly*, p. 54.